Tell Me
Exactly What
Happened

Tell Me Exactly What Happened

Dispatches from 911

Caroline Burau

MINNESOTA HISTORICAL SOCIETY PRESS

www.mnhspress.org
The Minnesota Historical Society Press is a member of the
Association of American University Presses.

Manufactured in the United States of America

10 9 8 7 6 5 4 3 2 1

♾ The paper used in this publication meets the minimum requirements
of the American National Standard for Information Sciences—
Permanence for Printed Library Materials, ANSI Z39.48-1984.

International Standard Book Number
ISBN: 978-1-68134-009-8 (paper)
ISBN: 978-1-68134-010-4 (e-book)

Library of Congress Cataloging-in-Publication Data
available upon request.

This and other Minnesota Historical Society Press books are
available from popular e-book vendors.

Tell Me Exactly What Happened
is set in the Dante typeface family.

Book design and typesetting by
BNTypographics West Ltd., Victoria, B.C. Canada

Printed by Versa Press, East Peoria, Illinois

"Although an act of help done timely might be small in nature,
it is truly larger than the world itself."

Thiruvalluvar, *Tirukural*

"There was a red button on the wall labelled EMERGENCY,
but no button labelled BEWILDERMENT."

Michel Faber, *The Book of Strange New Things*

Contents

Introduction

The first call I ever took as a 911 dispatcher was a theft from vehicle, I think. The first one that kept me up all night was a suicide. The hundreds and thousands of calls that I took in the twelve years that followed have become like jelly beans in a jar to me. They are not all the same, but they are not that different. The more I add, the heavier the jar becomes.

I'd like to put them away and forget about them sometimes. But like a true sugar fiend, I can't.

Not much has changed in 911 since that theft-from-vehicle call, on the surface.

Cities and counties still struggle to keep the balance between spending too much money on communications and not spending enough (and ending up on the evening news). Dispatchers still feel overworked, underappreciated, and poorly trained. Cell phones continue to replace land lines, making callers harder to locate. Crank calls are still a thing.

Yet, in the last twelve years, marathons, elementary schools, and private businesses have oddly become potential bombing targets. The terms "active shooter" and "homeland security" no longer need explaining to the average person.

The Internet has become a tool for both solving crime and committing it. Identity thieves and cyberbullies make it ever more possible for us to become victims without even leaving our homes.

It's now possible to text your emergent message to 911, and soon callers will be able to video chat with 911. (At this, I can hear the collective shudder of dispatchers everywhere. *I'm going to have to look . . . respectable?*)

I've changed a bit, too.

I have fewer zits and more gray hairs. I've found yoga and lost religion. I've raised a child. I've learned something new every single day on the job, whether I wanted to or not.

I've helped deliver two babies. I've listened to countless child death scenes.

I've lost coworkers to suicide.

I've helped save lives. I've listened to many more of them just slip away.

I've eaten more Culver's chicken strips than any one human ever should.

I've watched *Saturday Night Live* hundreds of times, but never once without interruption, and mostly on mute.

I've depended far too heavily on coffee and Benadryl.

I've worked with some of the finest, funniest, most caring assholes who've ever lived.

So, I find myself wanting to write about it, again. Not because the story of my dispatching career is so unique, but because it is not. Because if I tell you what it is like to answer 911 in White Bear Lake, Minnesota, I'm also telling you a lot about what it's like to answer 911 just about anywhere.

Dispatchers joke a lot about "job security." Sometimes job security means that we can always count on a healthy supply of stupidity out in the world to make the phone keep ringing. Sometimes it is a commentary on all of the different ways we humans can hurt ourselves and each other. Sometimes it's because we know most normal people won't work nights and weekends. But mostly, it just means that people will never stop needing help.

Dispatchers are listeners. They are also waiters. They wait for you to call, they wait for help to get to you, and they wait to find out if you are okay. They wait for cops to answer that they are okay, they wait for helicopters to land, and they wait for more phones to ring and start it all over again. They wait for you to hang up because they won't hang up on you. They wait to find out if it was as bad as it sounded. They wait for the end of their shifts. They wait to retire.

There is no beginning to this story, and no end. The dispatch center never closes and the phones never get shut off.

There is just call after call after life after death after life again. And so it goes. And we sit in our hot seats: listening, waiting, and answering 911.

NOTE: In order to protect the privacy of the men and women who've worked this job with me, I have made changes that will obscure their identities. In some cases, that means a name change. In others, it means names and identifying characteristics or contexts must change as well. I used as much or more caution to protect the callers and patients I write about. Some callers are a combination of two people. Some descriptions of people and conversations are purposely vague. I'm attempting to expose the way this job has affected me without exposing those I've met along the way.

I

Insomnia

I've just finished my second of two consecutive twelve-hour night shifts. My garage door is rising in front of me, and I have no memory of the twenty-five-minute drive that brought me to it.

My mom always gasps at the twelve-hour part like it is the first she's heard of it—"Such long shifts? How can you do that?" When really, I've been working the 5:00 P.M. to 5:00 A.M. shifts on and off for seven years. Some of my coworkers speak with nostalgia about the days when sixteen-hour shifts were still allowed. I can't fathom that.

I punch the code on the deadbolt and I'm in my mud room. It takes all of my attention to untie the laces on my boots. My polyester pants weigh twenty pounds.

I slowly take the layers of my job off of myself. I hang a black jacket with reflective letters on a coat rack. I remove my security badge lanyard from around my neck. I fumble at the buttons of my dingy white polyester work shirt. I let my hair out of its tie.

I think about a call I took around 1:00 A.M. Or was it 3:00 A.M.? A man with severe chest pain. He called me "Darlin'." Half drunk. I hope he's okay. Terms of endearment are rather uncommon in this line of work.

I think about a sixteen-year-old giving birth to her second child.

I think about helicopters flying across the state in the cold night. Souls on board.

Stab wounds.

Screaming toddlers.

Lights and sirens.

God damn it. At 4:40 A.M., when I was at my console watching actual seconds tick by, my entire being, everything that I was, had one desire: to fall asleep. To be in my bed. I was *daydreaming about sleeping.*

But now.

Power bills.

Vet appointments.

Sex. Money.

That last big fight with my husband, by text, around midnight.

Did I call my mom about dinner on Sunday?

Shit I can't do anything about right now.

These things crowd my brain like one hundred phone lines ringing all at once. No amount of fatigue seems able to mute them.

I can't sleep during the day.

Not really. Not in that restful, dreamy, moonlit state we all crave so much after age thirty. Just in a fretful way. It's as if no matter how tired my body is, my brain just can't believe it.

Somewhere along the line, I started taking one Benadryl after every night shift in the hopes that I could muster five or six hours of deep sleep before having to go back in. I've since graduated to two, yet it rarely works. I'll drift off around 6:00 or 7:00 A.M. only to find myself wide awake at 11:00 A.M.

Then I begin to fret. Will I get more sleep? Maybe I eat some cereal. Vacuum the carpet on the stairs, if nobody else is home. Masturbate. Check my e-mail. Pay a bill. Something . . . anything . . . to make my body and my mind agree to rest. To be able to say, *There. That's done, then. Now I can go to sleep.*

I calculate the hours as they slip by me. If I get to sleep again by noon, I could get another three hours before I have to get up. Okay, 1:00 P.M. then. If I get to sleep by 1 . . .

I might cry. Maybe a good cry will make me tired enough. I might cry over big or small things. My mother's chronic pain. The latest car repair. The death of the family cat.

I could cry over the fact that in less than three hours, I'll be back at the 911 console on four hours of sleep, sucking down coffee and aching from the pain of just having to be awake. Terrified of what I could miss and who that might let down. Dreading the downtime between each crisis almost as much as the calls themselves, knowing each way of passing the time has its own special hazards.

At 11:00 A.M., then noon, then 1:00 P.M., then 2:00 P.M., with the sun high in the sky, its beams angrily shooting through the seams in the blackout shades that had been so meticulously taped over the windows, I sometimes think about dying.

I think about the several hundred Benadryl in the bathroom cabinet (the more you buy, the more you save!), and I wonder just how many it would take. How many dozen would I need to finally, mercifully, get some rest? I even Googled it once: What is the lethal dose of Benadryl? Can one even overdose on an allergy med? I am too tired to make the effort. And too scared.

I stand outside those thoughts and watch myself process them. How bad does a person have to feel? How much exhaustion? My sponsor in AA would remind me to HALT! Meaning I've gone and let myself get too Hungry, Angry, Lonely, or Tired. *But I am halted,* I object to no one in particular. I'm suspended between awake and asleep, aching to truly be either one or the other. I'm halted and I'm *stuck.*

I search for a mantra from a yoga class that might lull me. I remember a chant from a restorative class that had what I thought at the time was a peaceful rhythm, back before it became the anthem of my insomnia.

"Wah-hey, guru, Wah-hey, guru, Wah-hey . . ."

I don't remember what it means, which is probably good. So, to me, it means nothing. Nothing is good. The idea is to push all other thoughts out of my head to make way for some nothing, some peace. But a few dozen wah-hey gurus later, I'm thinking about minutes and Benadryl again.

In the darkest moments, I laugh at myself. I laugh at my dark thoughts. *Some lifesaver you are.* I check the time on my phone for the thousandth time.

What now? Call 911?

～

Every day, I think about quitting this job.

Recently, I landed an interview for a "normal job." Since my degree is in print media, I often dream about leaving dispatch forever and writing ad or technical copy for a living. You know, non-emergent corporate stuff. Newsletters. Manuals. Work that can be completed between the hours of 8:00 A.M. and 5:00 P.M., Monday through Friday.

Heck, sometimes, when I'm sitting in the dark, noisy comm center, dispatching bar fights and heart attacks while all my friends are out doing Saturday night stuff, I get to the point where I'd haul trash if I had to, just for better hours. On those nights, I long to be one of those people who just *knows* that she's going to have Christmas off. Weekend barbeque? Sunday brunch? Of course I'll be there! *I don't work weekends.*

But, it's not just about weekends. Talking to a friend about the interview, he asked me the last question I ever want to ask myself about leaving 911: "Won't you miss doing something important?"

I tried to shrug that off. No. Because . . . weekends are important. Sleeping at night is important. Not having to listen to people die, people scream, people cry. That's important. My sanity. Super important. "It's not like I'm . . ."

"Last month you *saved a life*," he reminded me. I had gotten my first "Lifesaver" pin for coaching a caller through the Heimlich maneuver on an unconscious woman with meat stuck in her throat. I knew right away I'd done a decent job on that call, in that I'd gotten a non-breathing person breathing again. I'd waited for weeks to find out how she came through. When I learned she had made a full recovery, I grinned like a moron for days. I was *high*. *I saved a life.* (And I was going to get a lovely piece of paper that I could frame, that says *Caroline saved a life*. Or words to that effect.)

"Okay, yeah," I shrugged, trying to feign modesty while my inner peacock comically swelled with pride.

"You should tell them about that call," he insisted.

"I don't know if they're looking for lifesavers to write tech copy."

"Well, they should be," he said. "Just work it into the interview somewhere. 'Oh, you have a great dental plan? That's very interesting. Well, I saved a *motherfucking life*.'"

I didn't end up discussing my life-save at the interview. Maybe I should have. They never called me.

Part of me was relieved. In my tenth year, I saved a life. But I've also helped countless others, delivered babies on the phone, calmed suicidal callers, stopped the bleeding, comforted the grief-stricken. I'm fast, efficient, and confident in my abilities. My coworkers are my partners. They are the family I fight large and small battles with every day.

Some days I'm all in, other days I want out. Twelve years in 911. Twelve years of endlessly learning strange, new, awful truths about how we humans treat each other. Twelve years of lives NOT saved. I've heard people die. I've heard people try to kill each other. I've heard mothers scream their babies into the world; I've heard them wail as they watch them go. Three coworker suicides. I've cried into my headset more times than I could count. I've hyperventilated. I've picked my fingers raw. I've lost sleep. I've slept for days. I've seen therapists, chaplains. I've prayed. I've stopped praying.

Or I could write copy.

And have weekends off. Christmas by the fireplace.

No more hangnails. No more night shifts.

It sounds *delicious*.

It sounds boring as shit.

"911?"

"Hey, uh, my girlfriend and I were having sex, and I . . . I heard something snap."

"Tell me exactly what happened."

"My penis. I think I broke it."

"How can you tell?"

"It's not the first time I've done this."

2

Small-Town Dispatcher

White Bear Lake, Minnesota, is my hometown. It is a first-ring suburb of St. Paul, twin city to Minneapolis. About 24,000 people live in White Bear Lake, and you can add another 11,000 for White Bear Township, also served by the White Bear Lake Fire Department.

I spent my childhood sleeping and waking in a house that was rarely ever locked. I put miles and miles on my Daisy Wheels bicycle (with the big yellow "banana seat") every summer, checking in with my mom only when I got hungry or needed a towel to go swimming at the public dock. I showed up a little bit after dark after a day of adventure, ready to hit the sack and start my idyllic little suburban life all over again the next day.

When it came time to decide where my husband Jim, my daughter Mariah, and I would stop renting and settle down, I insisted on moving back to White Bear Lake. I wanted to be close to my parents, who still lived in the same 1920s two-story where they'd raised me. So as far as I knew when I took my two years of county dispatching experience and transferred them over to the White Bear Lake Police Department, White Bear Lake was a *nice, quiet town.*

And it still is a *nice, quiet town,* if you're strolling through Matoska Park, watching sailboats meander from one end of the lake to the other. Or if you're sitting on a bench in downtown, enjoying a hand-dipped ice cream from Cup 'n Cone.

But not necessarily if you're sitting in White Bear Lake's one-person dispatch center.

"911?"

"Hi, I live on County Road F, and the house down the street just . . . basically . . . exploded."

"I'm watching my neighbor beat up on his girlfriend in their front yard. You guys know him. You know him. He's a *big guy*. You better get over here. He's going to kill her."

"I'm at the Lifetime Fitness and I just watched someone drive my car out of the parking lot!"

"I think the guy next door is cooking meth. It smells terrible, all the time. Really, like, nuclear-war terrible."

"I just slapped my sixteen-year-old son. He called his mom a 'bitch,' and I slapped him. We need to talk to somebody."

The house? Gas explosion. No fatalities.

The girlfriend? She lived.

The car? We caught up to the bad guys (teenagers) and recovered it.

The meth? I don't know.

The dad, the kid, and the mom? They'll be fine. (Sergeant said the kid had it coming.)

If you're into watching reality shows about 911, you may think we take "home invasion" calls all the time, or that we're constantly taking calls from little children barely old enough to speak and helping them save their mothers. Or that every other call is a suicidal person or a near-fatal domestic argument. But those are just the calls that make for the best audio and that make the most interesting reenactments.

Often, it's not the nature of the calls we take that causes our gray hairs, stress-eating, and general surly dispositions. It's the *volume* of those calls and the speed at which we must deal with them. Imagine that every fifteen minutes or so, someone comes racing into your workplace with a crossword puzzle, slams it on your desk, and says,

"The longer you take to finish this, the longer somebody else might suffer or even die!"

Imagine that every so often, you get two or three of those puzzles on your desk at a time.

My workplace, the dispatch center, was a well-secured fishbowl in the center of the police and fire building. In the center of the center at a large console sat the lone dispatcher. The chair faced the front lobby, open twenty-four hours a day.

Slightly blocking my view of the well-windowed lobby were two large monitors that usually displayed maps of White Bear Lake and the locations of the officers on duty represented by tiny, cartoonish squad-car icons labeled with their tiny little squad numbers. (At White Bear, all officers are assigned numbers in the 300s. The dispatcher's number is always 300.)

Thanks to this new-at-the-time technology, if I dispatched squad number 323 to a call, and if I was impatient for him to get there, I could watch his little vehicle make the slow crawl across the map to his destination in real time. If he took a weird route, I could ask him if he was lost and needed directions. But I can't advise that last bit. Not all who wander are lost; they may just be trying to finish lunch.

Next to the main console sat yet another computer and monitor on a smaller desk. This setup was for entering and searching "data." License data, offender data, stolen vehicles, etc.

All around me, more windows. The large window to my left gave me a full view of the records office and anyone in it. To my right, a service window where officers could stop and chat, or pass things to me under the glass. Ideally, they passed me treats given them by members of the grateful public. Mostly, it was just information about stolen items or missing children that I then had to enter into the database.

Behind me, a supervisor's office and a security door. Just beyond the security door, a bathroom with a backup phone—for when urgency and emergency collided.

I had one standard-issue headset, but there was also a good, old-fashioned, desk phone–style receiver, which I used the most. It allowed me the freedom to just jump up and talk to someone at the lobby window without being tethered to the desk. I could even walk around the console while still on the phone, stretching the generosity of the long, curly cord, just like a 1980s teenager on the family phone.

On the wall, a large-faced digital clock advertised the time, which was handy since we ended all of our transmissions with a time stamp.

"300 to 323, do you need directions to that call?"

"Negative, 300, I can get there *just fine*."

"Copied! 16:24."

All in all, a pretty decent setup for multitasking, communicating, and, of course, saving the world.

～

"911?"

"Hi, there's a guy unconscious out on the lake and he just got thrown off his jet ski."

"Where on the lake are you?"

My caller is on a cell phone, as anyone would be if calling from a boat, so I don't have an exact address, just a set of coordinates that gets me within a few blocks of him, that is if those coordinates are correct, which they often are not.

"I don't know. I can see a red house with dormers."

"Do you know what street you are close to? Are you close to a boat landing or a beach?"

Let me just note that it is perfectly natural to want to tell the dispatcher about the red house with dormers. Thanks to TV shows like CSI, most well-meaning, taxpaying folks think that we actually have a database that will quickly generate a list of every red house with dormers in the county, and if it's lakefront property of course. Or maybe this guy just thinks I know the area *that well*.

"We launched from Matoska Park."

"Where are you from there?"

"Um, to the right?"

"East or west of there?"

"I don't know! To the right. Whatever direction that is."

Are you getting impatient for me to see about the unconscious guy on the lake? Me too, but I haven't really solved the location riddle to my satisfaction.

Still, I make a judgment call and enter a call for the Matoska boat landing, key the main channel, and say, "300 to 334 and 356."

To my caller, I say, "Can you get him out of the water? Can you reach him?"

"I don't know."

Radio: "334 here."

"Aaaand 356."

"Both squads, I need you for a possible drowning on White Bear Lake." I get them started code 3 (lights and sirens) to Matoska Park, where they will undoubtedly arrive and start asking me where the hell this poor guy is.

"Do the best you can," I plead to my caller. "It's going to be a few minutes until we get there."

Now I need to put him on hold and call Ramsey County to start Water Patrol. On a busy Saturday afternoon, there's bound to be a deputy out on the lake who can get there quicker. (Plus, the water is actually their jurisdiction, not ours.)

Still, I hate that I had to put the caller *on hold*. I can almost hear Leah McLean (or someone equally perky) on *5 Eyewitness News:* "Tonight at ten: Listen as a local resident calls 911 for help with a drowning man, and the operator *puts him on hold!*"

Two rings at Ramsey County before a female dispatcher picks up. It feels like two minutes.

"What direction from Matoska Park?" she asks me.

"Um, to the right."

"To the right?"

"I have two officers on the way. Hopefully I'll have more for you soon," I add with an appropriately apologetic tone. *Would you like to hear about the dormers?*

I should also get the fire department going. I should also grow another head and another two hands. But even if I did, I guess I'd still have only one phone and one radio in front of me.

And then another 911 line rings (because it's a sunny Saturday afternoon).

"911?"

"Hi. My seventeen-year-old has been gone since Thursday and I want to file a report."

"Okay, can you hold?"

"Uh, I guess so."

("Desperate mom calls 911 about her missing son, and the operator puts her on hold!")

I quickly punch the first 911 to get my guy on the lake, but find that he has disconnected.

"334 to 300, I'm arrived, and looking. Do you have a better location for this?"

I am already dialing the cell number back at that moment. One ring. Two, three, four, and voicemail.

Another try, and another voicemail.

"334, I'm getting no answer on the call back."

"Dispatch, you can disregard. Patient is located and out of the water."

I'm going to go ahead and *not* ask how long he has known this.

"Copy, patient is out of the water. Cancel fire?"

"Negative. Keep them coming for an eval. Code 2."

I slow the fire department on the radio and wait for one medic, one engine, and one ambulance to copy my transmission.

A non-emergent line rings.

"WhiteBearLakePoliceandFire, is this an emergency?"

"Um, no. Not really."

Hallelujah! Because I've still got that missing-kid call on hold. Plus I have to cancel Water Patrol. Neither party is bound to be super happy with me. Both have decent reasons. I'm holding out hope that this non-emergent line I've got on hold is someone who likes me. Or isn't currently irritated with me. That would be delicious.

Fifteen minutes later, I realize that after answering and dispatching a medical call, I still never canceled Water Patrol.

"It's fine," the dispatcher snaps when I finally get through. "We heard the squads cancel on your main channel."

Translated: *We were monitoring your radios, and once again were able to do your job for ya. Slacker.*

Le sigh.

So, what happened on the lake? Was the patient ever really unconscious? Was there really a jet ski? Was it alcohol-related? Was the caller his good friend or just a passerby? Were they to the left or the right of Matoska Park?

I might never know. If 334 comes in later to shoot the shit or ask me to enter something stolen into the statewide database, maybe I will ask. Or maybe I'll have taken ten more calls that made me forget all about it.

"911?"

"Hi, I'd like to report what sounds like gunfire in my backyard."

"Can you see anyone?"

"No, I'm afraid to look."

"Does it maybe sound like . . . fireworks?"

"It . . . maybe. Are you going to send someone?"

"On July 3? No, ma'am."

3

Somebody in Charge

When I joined White Bear Lake in 2005, the 911 community in Ramsey County was all abuzz with merger talk.

"It's never going to happen," my boss, Mack Lyttle, assured during my first month on the job. "People like their Mayberry just the way it is." Maybe he thought it was something I wanted to hear, since I'd just left Ramsey County less than a year before. But I wasn't so sure.

Mergers are the Walmarting of 911. It's not that Walmart is all bad. Anyone who's ever needed a lawn chair, a screwdriver, a dozen eggs, and some pink thread all at the same time has to admit that Walmart is *not all bad*.

But White Bear Lake is a proud town. It's a second-ring suburb of St. Paul, one of the suburbs in the metro area with a history that goes further back than that of its own first strip mall. F. Scott Fitzgerald once summered with his wife Zelda at the White Bear Lake Yacht Club. Gangsters John Dillinger, Ma Barker, and her boys hung out on the east side of the lake.

White Bear Lake was a suburb with a "downtown" long before downtowns were cool. The police department is, of course, downtown. If you want to talk to someone about your missing cat or your neighbor's yard full of dead deer carcasses or your out-of-control mother-in-law, you can walk into the lobby any time of day or night, 365 days a year, and talk to a real live person about it. A dispatcher, to be specific. If he or she isn't on the phone.

Parts of me hoped really hard that White Bear Lake would join that merger. If we merged, I'd have partners again. Partners to save me from putting people on hold. Partners to keep me from forgetting to cancel Water Patrol. Partners to order fast food with. Laugh with! Cry with! I could go on. But if White Bear Lake was to merge with the big county, that old-timey walk-up customer service would go away forever.

Keeping a walk-up window often meant that I had to be in two places at once. The phone and radio were actually several paces from the window. It didn't help matters that we dispatchers looked just like cops. Our uniforms were essentially identical to the uniform our officers wore, minus the duty belt with all the fun toys, like guns and handcuffs. (I lived in fear that I'd someday find myself at a Subway before work in my cop uniform, and someone would come in with a gun and try to rob the place. I envisioned the customers and the sandwich artists looking to me to do something brave and cop-like, as I curled up into the fetal position and covered my head. I brown-bagged it a lot.)

So even though the patch on my arm said "Communications," most folks who came to my window assumed I was an officer.

"We need your help with an issue," a stout, bearded man said to me one night. He had come rushing in with a woman not far behind him. Both seemed breathy and sweaty.

"What can I help you with?"

"We have a domestic issue we want to report."

"Okay. If you want to take a seat, I can page an officer . . ."

"See, my wife thinks it's okay to see her ex every day, talk to him on the phone . . . all this fucking bullshit . . ."

"You don't know what the fuck you're talking about!"

Oh, I get it. You are *the domestic issue you wish to report.*

"What the . . . don't I know what the fuck I'm talking about?" Angry spittle coated the man's facial hair, and I was reminded for the hundredth time why I liked the security glass so very much.

"I'm so fucking sick of your shit!" his significant other yelled, inexplicably moving herself closer to the angry-spittle zone.

"Sir and ma'am!" I yelled authoritatively.

They both turned to me. That's it. That's all I had to contribute. *What do I look like, a marriage counselor? I'm not even the thing I actually do look like.*

I backed away abruptly, rushed to my radio console, keyed the mic, and said, "I need any available officer to the lobby for a walk-in domestic."

Mack quickly chimed in from his office, and I breathed a sigh of relief.

"300, there's a domestic . . . in the lobby?"

"Affirm. Please help. Like, code 3. The fur, it's flying."

"Copy. En route."

~

One afternoon, someone came to our twenty-four-hour lobby with an apparent . . . bomb.

When folks enter the police department lobby during normal business hours, they have two choices. They can lean right and go to the administrative window and talk to a records clerk. Otherwise, they can lean left and talk to a dispatcher.

It was a weekday afternoon before 5:00 P.M., but she chose my window anyway. It wasn't her first time there. As I maneuvered my way around my L-shaped desk so I could talk to her, she took a quick, nervous glance over her shoulder.

"Can I talk to somebody in charge?" she said timidly.

"What can I help you with?" I asked.

"I'm Tina LaCrosse," she said, and I recognized her name from the many violent domestic situations our officers had interrupted at her home. She didn't outwardly look like someone whose life was a swirling ball of chaos, with her neatly straightened hair and magenta manicure. Still.

"My ex-husband sent me a package."

She described it to me. She hadn't opened it expecting a box of kittens (live kittens, anyway), but once she did, she was pretty concerned about what she saw. Wires.

"I guess it could be a bomb," she said, eyes wide.

"Where is it?" I asked, backing away slightly.

"In there." She gestured behind her. In . . . where? In the building? You know what? Never mind. Time to find that *in-charge* person she's asking about.

I maneuvered back around to the false security of my radio console.

"312."

"312?"

Thank merciful heavens. I could tell from the feedback that Sergeant Gregory was in the building somewhere and, oddly, seemed to already know that I had something special cooking in the lobby.

"Come to dispatch please." *Super fast, Sarg. Pretty please with sugar on top.*

"Copy. I'm en route on that . . . detail."

Turns out, another officer had intercepted her out in the parking lot, and *the package* had already been brought to our fingerprinting room, which is *just off the front lobby*. If I had been consulted, I would have suggested other locations *to place a bomb*. (Note: Dispatchers tend to be non-sworn civilians, and thereby rarely consulted on matters of bomb placement.)

Things started happening really quickly.

The bomb squad was called. And the police chief, and the fire chief, and the city manager. Since the fire and police departments and city hall both occupy the same city block, everyone in both buildings had to be evacuated. I watched many of them slowly file out through our large glass double doors as my phones kept ringing.

Nobody was telling me to evacuate, but I was open to hearing it.

If I stood at the lobby window and leaned out a bit, I could actually see the suspicious box with the wires resting peacefully on a table in the fingerprinting room. The building slowly became more and more empty. But my phones kept ringing.

My supervisor, a soft-spoken and studious man with wire-rimmed glasses, had been working steadily for ten minutes, trying to roll our phone lines into Ramsey County's phones so that he and I could also leave, but it was slow going.

And the phones . . . well, you know.

"Hey, uh, Jeff?" I said with a bit more of an edge than I had intended. "How much longer?"

"I'm working on it," he replied.

These things just don't happen very often. Shortly after the attacks of September 11, much lip service was given about building and maintaining backup communications centers, or what this or that big city department might do if its building was attacked, etc. But when it comes down to it, what you don't practice frequently eventually gets lost in the minutia of our everyday false alarms. And frankly, I don't think any of us ever imagined that anyone would find a city like White Bear Lake to be, well, all that *bomb-worthy*.

More than anything, I was just glad Jeff was on site when little Miss *Does-this-look-like-a-bomb?* came in. I knew he'd get us out of that dispatch center. I just didn't know quite *when*.

"356 to 300."

356 was calling me. But I wasn't sure if I wanted to answer. At some point in all of this, I'd begun to wonder something disturbing: if I key the mic or answer the phone, *is that going to spark something?* Is it going to set something off? Perhaps it was a real concern. Perhaps it was the product of watching too many episodes of *MacGyver* and *The A-Team* as a child.

I timidly moved my index finger to the transmit button, imagining a slow-motion scene in some late '80s action film, where the simple touching of this red button could detonate a bomb.

"3 . . . 56. Go ahead."

"Just checking your location," 356 said angrily.

What a strange role reversal, to have an officer checking *my* location. He was sending a message to Jeff, who heard it loud and clear.

"Just a few more minutes," he assured me. Okay, but if we get blown up, 356 is going to be *really pissed at us*.

Presently, I heard a whirr, and caught something moving out of the corner of my eye.

It was a bomb robot, heading slowly and awkwardly into the fingerprinting room. I couldn't tell who was controlling it, or from where. Was it going to poke the box? Make it mad? Drop it? Sweet hell in a handbasket.

356, nobody up in here but me, Jeff, and R2D2.

"356, we'll be out shortly."

"Copy."

Mercifully, the phones were actually fairly quiet in those long minutes. Nothing emergent, and nothing requiring me to page out the fire department or stay on the line for very long. But still, they rang.

"911?"

"I don't have the non-emergency number, but my car was impounded last night, and I need to find out where it went."

"What city was it towed from?"

"Vadnais Heights."

"Let me transfer you."

Ironically, it was one for Ramsey County.

"Caroline!" I turned to see the White Bear Lake chief of police standing at the service window outside the dispatch center. She was a stout, no-nonsense woman who looked equally ready for either a high-pressure press conference or a foot chase involving an armed felon, whichever presented itself first. She was the kind of person you want in charge. She was the kind of person who could look you right in the eye and tell you exactly what you needed to hear to keep you going in a tough situation. Even if it's bullshit.

"You're perfectly safe in there," she said authoritatively. "All of the glass is shatterproof. Don't worry about anything, okay? You will be just fine."

"Okay, Chief, thank you!"

She marched off, returning, I assume, to the staging area two blocks away.

The truth is, nobody was making me stay. Jeff offered several times to take over, despite how busy he already was. But how could I leave? This was the type of situation I sent officers and firefighters into all the time. Total uncertainty. Was it a bomb? Was it a clock radio? Did R2D2 know what the hell he was doing? I figured it was good for me. It felt strangely fitting for me to be so far out of my comfort zone, *while sitting in my comfort zone.*

Still, tick tock.

I resisted the urge to do a web search on the terms *shatterproof* versus *bombproof.* I resisted the urge to call my daughter and husband and tell them I loved them. Mainly, I just didn't want to touch any more damn buttons than I had to.

"312 to 300."

Okay, will everybody please stop making me touch buttons now?

"312, go ahead."

"Come meet me at the back entrance and I'll take you to staging."

But, Jeff? *Wait. Where the hell did he go?*

"I'll be just another minute," Jeff said from behind me.

"Really?"

"Yep, county's got the phones now."

"Roger copy," I said, grabbing my purse. Over and out.

The sun was shining brightly when I exited the building, and I hugged the sergeant's bulletproof vest the moment I saw him.

"Careful not to talk too loudly," he told me as we made our way toward the rest of my coworkers. "The media is starting to show up."

But as with most things that we deal with, the big deal was not a big deal. The bomb was not a bomb. It was a clock radio . . . or something. I don't remember, actually. What I remember most about that day was how very freaking long twenty minutes can last.

In 2007, for better or for worse, when all of the other cities of Ramsey County merged their public-safety communications into one location in St. Paul, the city of White Bear Lake declined. And for better or for worse, the lobby remains open twenty-four hours a day, 365 days a year, to anyone who wishes to talk to somebody in charge.

"911?"

"Hey, can you tell me what was going on over on Country Road E and Highland last Monday? Around five-ish?"

"I can try. What did you see?"

"There were like five squad cars sitting at that brown house, so it must have been something big."

"I'm not finding anything in my database around that time."

"You must have something!"

"They went for a possible felony warrant, but it looks like they were only there for a few minutes. So the guy with the warrant must have left or something."

"So, I pay my taxes so cops can sit around and do nothing?"

Yes, that's exactly what I meant. Glad we're communicating.

"The more officers that can respond, the safer they are."

"But five? That's ridiculous."

Unless you're one of those cops, I guess.

"Is there anything else I can help you with?"

4

Permission to Pee Denied

"911?"

"Yeah, my name is Bob Dunham, and I'm calling about my son. See, two years ago, he moved back in with us from Texas, and when he first got here, he would drink a little bit here and there, but nothing too serious . . ."

"Okay, what's the problem?"

"Well, he had this girlfriend, and they broke up last week, and she's no slouch either, in the drinking department . . ."

"Are they having an argument?"

"No. She's not here. Well, to make a long story short . . ."

"Sir, what's the problem today? What are you calling 911 about?"

"Well, I'm trying to tell you."

"Is there something going on with your son right now?"

"Well, yeah! He's in the bathroom saying he wants to kill himself."

Sheesh.

"And you're at 3700 High Crest?"

"Yes."

"And does he have a weapon?"

"He owns a gun, but I think he just has a pocketknife in there."

"Okay, I'm going to get someone started right now. Don't hang up. Okay?"

(When I hear recordings of my calls, I find that I say "okay" a lot. Maybe I'm just trying to make things okay by the power of suggestion?)

"320, 323."

"320 here."

"323."

"Need you both to respond code 3 to 3700 High Crest . . ."

"300? 344. I'm on the south end. That'll be mine."

"Copy, 320, you can cancel and I'll show 344 and 323 en route to High Crest."

Dangit. Dangit. Dangit.

Officer Brenna Gunderson is one cop on a very short list of cops who feel comfortable enough at the dispatch console to cover me while I take a bathroom break. I wouldn't say any of them *like* sitting there, but some hate it less than others. Brenna used to dispatch in a neighboring county, so she knows what it means not to be in charge of her own bathroom breaks, and she frequently takes pity on me.

Because sometimes—unless you're a camel—you just have to pee.

I actually had to pee about two thefts and one medical before Mr. Long Story Short called, but I was trying to maneuver 344 to the north end of the city without announcing to the whole world that I had to pee. This was before I realized that UTIs are actually much more uncomfortable than routine embarrassments about bodily functions.

It's not that I *have* to wait for her. There's actually a bathroom just steps away from me, across the hall. There's even a phone right next to the throne if someone calls midstream, and a portable radio in case a cop tries to reach me.

But it doesn't matter because now I've got two cops headed to a suicidal with a weapon, I've got the suicidal's dad on the phone, and the world just doesn't seem to give two shits about the fact that I have to pee.

When I first started this job, most calls still freaked me out enough that my adrenaline would kick in and shut off the urgency for a while. There are still some calls that will do that, but not this one.

I'm not scared, I'm not jazzed, and I'm not even kidding. I just plain—have to pee.

"344."

"344?" *Chop-chop. Mamma's drowning up in here.*

"I'm on scene with his parents."

"Copied, 20:36."

"323."

"323 on scene?"

"Roger."

The toilet beckons, but I know it's still too soon. I can't just walk away. Ironically, we need to get one suicidal off a toilet before I can get *on a toilet.*

Minutes tick by. I mentally flog myself for that last cup of coffee. What was I thinking? *Take fluids on your own time, missy!*

"344, 10-23?"

That's ten-code for "How's it going over there?"

"Stand by."

Sure thing. Take all the time you need. No, really.

"300 we're 10-24 with the subject. We'll be here for a while though."

"344, I copied."

"10-24" means "We're okay for now, but keep the status checks coming."

The other part means my relief is not going to make it back before I piddle the carpet like an elderly pug, so it's time for me to just grab a portable and hope for the best.

I prop the security door open (which we are not supposed to do), set the portable down on the tank (which also feels like a bad idea, but the sink isn't big enough), and lock the door.

Oh, sweet relief! Oh, precious moment of solitude! Oh . . .

"300, 344."

I will hurt you, 344. I don't care that you are an officer of the law. I will hunt you down and wait until you have to use the facilities, and I will handcuff you to your own pig rig.

I stop peeing. I'm a lot of things, but I'm *not* a dispatcher who pees while transmitting on the main channel.

"344, go." I say it nice and slow so that the echo of the bathroom walls can be heard loud and clear.

"300, we're going to need a BLS [basic life support crew] routine for a mental-health eval."

"Copied. I'll page them . . . shortly."

"Uh, thank you."

"20:45."

One thing I can't do from the biff is page out the fire department. I resume peeing. The second half of my three-minute break is— mercifully—uninterrupted.

Half an hour later, Brenna bursts in code 3, and with a concerned look on her face.

"I'm sorry I took so long!" she nearly bellows. "I'm here to relieve you!"

She's just come from a stranger's home to which I had sent her, talked a suicidal man into putting a knife down, and then convinced him to get help. And now she's apologizing to *me*.

I'm *such a dink*.

"It's all good," I sigh. "It's . . . taken care of."

"You peed your pants?"

"Ha-ha."

"But, have you had a break yet tonight?"

"No, but it's been pretty dead." *Up until the part where it wasn't.*

"Take a break now! I'm here. Take a walk or something. Do it! Come on. Do it. Do it."

"Okay." I reluctantly push myself into a standing stretch. "That theft in the pending queue can wait for the next shift."

"Roger copy. Now go!"

I make my way toward the door, but I'm startled by a high whining noise coming from Brenna's face.

"Take a portable, please!" she wheezes dramatically.

"Oh, right." I grab one and hold it up reassuringly before I finally turn toward the door. I forgot how frightening that console can be when you don't work it all the time.

"You'll be fine," I tell her, patting her on her WBPD patch. "You just disarmed a dude. Probably did some kung fu stuff on him, too. This is nothing."

"Don't go far!"

"Yes, Officer."

"911?"

"There's a guy walking down the street in a trench coat with some kind of long weapon."

"Okay, where is he now?"

"He's walking up McKnight near the school."

"Near south campus? The high school?"

"Yeah."

"Okay, stay on the line while I page . . ."

"I'm not there anymore."

"Where are you?"

"I'm going to work. This was about five minutes ago. Just thought you should know."

5

A Whiff of Ammonia

Sometimes, we get "sit-alongs" in dispatch. This means that someone has come in to hang out and see what the job is like, for whatever reason. Maybe a law-enforcement student has to sit for a few hours to satisfy a requirement, or maybe it's somebody who wants to see if they're cut out for the job.

The thing about sit-alongs is that they cause the world to stop needing 911 for as long as they're sitting there.

A sit-along is an awkward event if the dispatcher and the sitter don't know each other, which is usually the case. You're sitting close enough to smell each other's breath, examine each other's nose hairs, that sort of thing. And you want a diversion to break the tension. You want something to talk about. You want call after call after burg in progress after stabbing after foot chase.

(There are times when emergency services folks will express the desire for increased business. We realize this makes us sound like we actually *want bad things to happen*. We really don't. We just know that *bad things happen*. And if they have to happen, we sometimes wish these things could happen exactly when we are ready and willing to deal with them. *Which, of course, never happens.*)

You want to show this person how busy we can actually get, how high it all piles up. You want them to leave and tell their friends: "Wow. Those dispatchers work their unexpectedly fit little butts off." You want to say things like, "Copy, one at gunpoint," and

"Affirmative, 332, we've got air en route." You want the phones to light up so you can show your sit-along what a badass, call-taking, squad-sending, life-saving mofo you are!

Instead, what you often get is some poor soul sitting just on the edge of your personal bubble, bored out of his (or her) gourd, and powerless to do anything but stare at the screen full of little toy squad cars resting peacefully in their positions on a map. Maybe your sit-along thinks up a couple of good questions, and you draw out your answers as long as humanly possible. Maybe a line lights up, and you grab it before the first ring even finishes. Maybe it's a double shooting or a fully engulfed house! No. It's a stupid old parking complaint.

You picture the sit-along telling friends: "Wow, those dispatchers are livin' the high life."

Oh, and the moment your sit-along walks out the door? Two at gunpoint. Ten-car pileup! It never fails.

Unless.

Unless your sit-along is someone you know, and this sit-along really isn't for educational purposes, but to shoot the shit with an old friend with minimal interruption.

Social sit-alongs are tricky because, technically, they're not supposed to exist. Officially, unauthorized personnel are not allowed in the dispatch center. Unofficially, after 5:00 P.M. and on weekends, when the chiefs, captains, and various muckety-mucks are away, things relax a little. Feet go up onto consoles, shirts go untucked, and friends stop by.

My social sit-along was actually a dispatcher, which felt somehow less policy-bending than other possible sit-alongs. Lily was a Ramsey County dispatcher and my first trainer. She and I could lose an hour easily, just chatting about raising daughters, or yoga, or the latest gossip on other cops and dispatchers we'd worked with. She had always known that White Bear Lake was a one-person center but had never seen it for herself. She was curious. It was a Saturday evening in mid-August. Generally, Saturdays stay slow until midnight, so I was looking forward to catching up with her.

Just as I saw her smiling face at the double doors of the police department lobby, a 911 line lit up. I gestured toward the receiver to let her know I was picking up a call (as if she couldn't have pieced that together).

"911?"

"Yeah, we need an ambulance over here at Morningstar, you know, Highway 61? We got a guy over here . . . he got a whiff of ammonia."

"Okay, we'll get them started. Is he awake?"

"Yeah, he's okay. But we need someone over here."

"Okay, sir, hold the line for a moment?"

Let me give you a little backstory about me that will make the rest of this call easier to understand: *I'm a dumbass.*

What my caller said: "He got a whiff of ammonia."

What I heard: "He's got pneumonia."

Ammonia: A highly flammable, colorless gas that, if inhaled, can cause severe damage to the throat and lungs.

Pneumonia: A condition considerably less serious than inhaling ammonia.

I buzzed Lily in through the first security door, then proceeded to dispatch one officer and one ambulance for a *pneumonia patient.*

Officer Nick Morgan was first to arrive at Morningstar Foods. Morningstar is a dairy-processing plant that, until that night, I had never heard of. It sits inconspicuously along Highway 61 at the western border of White Bear Lake (behind a Dairy Queen, coincidentally). In my five months on the job, I had never dispatched a call there. That is the beginning and ending of my defense of the acute dumbassery I exhibited that night.

Plants like Morningstar often use ammonia in their refrigeration systems. And I know that now.

Nick entered the building without anything even resembling a clear picture of what was going on at Morningstar, and when he did, he also got a whiff of ammonia. Much later, after the chaos of that evening was mostly over, he would begin to feel sick. He was taken to the hospital and, mercifully, released without serious injury. But I will always feel responsible for that.

I buzzed Lily in through the second security door. We hugged. She mentioned something about a funny smell in the air approaching the city hall along Highway 61.

Then all hell broke loose.

"337 to dispatch."

Officer Morgan's radio voice was generally very clipped and businesslike, but this was the clippiest I'd ever heard him.

"Go ahead," I replied casually.

"300, this is an *ammonia* leak. Page the fire department, all-call."

Just like it sounds, "all-call" means *send everyone. Right the heck now.*

"Well, there ya have it," Lily said matter-of-factly.

Across the western part of the city, folks began to smell it, too. And they began to call in to talk to me about it. Meanwhile, the men and women of our volunteer fire department had gotten their all-call pages and began to check in with me on the main channel or by phone. And since it was a warm mid-August night, and I am just one person, I slowly began to get my *dumb ass* handed to me.

"WhiteBearLakePoliceandFirecanyoupleasehold?"

"WhiteBearLakePoliceandFirecanyoupleasehold?"

"WhiteBearLakePoliceandFirecanyoupleasehold?"

I glanced at Lily, who seemed to know what I was about to ask, but still needed me to ask it.

"Could you start grabbing lines?" I said, panicky.

"Yup!" she said, picking up the receiver of the spare phone that sat between us. She'd saved my ass dozens of times at Ramsey County, and she was about to do it once again, at a dispatch center she didn't even work in, with only the approval of someone who had *zero authority.*

Then, the media got wind *(see what I did there?)* of the ammonia leak.

Talking to the media is a bit like picking up a sales call from a credit-card company. If your goal is to end the call politely, you can have that *eventually*. But they're going to make you work for it.

"Hi! This is Chris O'Blah from Channel Blah! Tell me about this chemical leak going on in your city!"

Well, Chris O'Blah, it's a real fucking hoot. And I've been hoping you would call, because I've got nothing but time to tell you all about it.

"I'm going to have to take your number and have our sergeant call you back when he's clear."

"Okay, but can you tell me if anyone is injured?"

"Your number please?"

"Are you putting the area on lockdown?"

Only media dinks say shit like "lockdown," by the way.

"I need your number." *And also some preemptive Advil.*

Once the Morningstar building, the Dairy Queen, and the nearby Texaco gas station were evacuated, officers began blocking off busy Highway 61 and adjacent side streets. This meant a major inconvenience for motorists, and therefore a new surge of phone calls to ask or complain about it.

A few callers were really upset that they couldn't access the Dairy Queen. I get it; I do.

"I don't know how long it's going to be blocked off," I told caller after caller. Nor could I answer their concerns about what would happen if they breathed too much of that chemical that I couldn't even properly pronounce just an hour earlier.

Much to the chagrin of the officers working the scene, I paged Mack Lyttle (our media liaison and my boss) about the goings-on at Morningstar. This was the kind of thing Mack lived for: big-time drama and the chance to have his handsome mug on the evening news. Some cops and dispatchers gave him flack for that, yet all of us were happy it was his job and not ours.

Since he didn't like recorded lines, Mack preferred to bleep me on the dispatch Nextel phone, which operates like a walkie-talkie and existed, apparently, because there weren't enough devices for the dispatcher to answer already.

So, on top of the phones and the radios, I had Lyttle calling me for updates for most of his twenty-minute commute to the scene.

"Dispatch."

"Stand by, Captain."

"Dispatch, can you read?"

Nobody says that, Mack.

"I copy you. Stand by."

"Dispatch, I'm ten minutes out."

"Copy that." *You knucklehead.*

"Dispatch."

"Yeah?"

"You doing okay in there?"

Mack was occasionally able to sense when he was tap-dancing on my very last nerve.

"Treading water. But I have some help."

"Copy. Let me know if you need anything."

In the end, more than seventy emergency workers responded to the call I first thought was a *guy with a fever.* Four people, including Officer Morgan, were treated and released at the local hospital, and the whole kit and caboodle was over in about two hours.

Two really long hours.

If Lily had been contemplating a job at White Bear Lake PD, she never followed through on it.

"911?"

"Yes, the power is out in my neighborhood . . ."

"Yes, ma'am, we are getting a lot of calls . . ."

"Well, when is it going to be back on?"

"I don't know, but I can give you the number for the power company."

"Okay, but can you tell me what happened?"

"I don't know just . . ."

"You don't know?"

"Okay . . . it's, uh, probably a busted flux capacitor."

"Oh, that sounds serious. Well, thank you."

"You're very welcome."

6

Regarding a Death

I met White Bear Lake Police Captain J. W. Lyttle about four years before I started working for him as a dispatcher. Everybody called him Mack. I was a reporter at the *White Bear Press* and he was my "media liaison," which is just a fancy way of saying that if anything big happened, crime-wise, in White Bear Lake, I had to call Mack for the scoop. Which worked out well, because he *loved* to talk.

In his corner window office at the PD, I met him once a week (or more if something big happened between Mondays). On his desk and wall were photos of him in his younger years, as a street cop in Florida. Often, a conversation about a strong-arm robbery at a gas station in White Bear Lake would drift to a long yarn about a drug deal gone bad in Port St. Lucie, or a foot chase he had been in, or a kidnapped child he'd helped recover.

I got the impression, at times, that he was full of shit. When he told me something outrageous, I'd make sure to take it down word for word and attribute it to him in print. His best, most incredible material was usually prefaced with the words ". . . but that's completely off the record, you understand?" And I'd have to put my pen down, smile, and just listen.

He was a consummate cop, suspicious of anything anyone told him. He received most information with a wry "I'll take that under advisement" look on his tanned face. Once, I came in with a bruise on my arm. He asked me how I got it, and I shrugged. I'm always running into things, I told him. I had no idea where or even when I'd gotten that one. "You sure about that?" he asked me, stone-cold serious.

"Yeah!" I laughed. For a moment (or possibly forever), he thought I was a battered wife.

He was a short, handsome flirt of a man with graying hair and broad shoulders. He was extremely proud of his girlfriend, Mia, a former White Bear Lake cop. When he spoke about her, his chest came out and his voice dropped low and he could become very serious. His children lived with his ex in Florida.

Mack frequently wiped his face with hand sanitizers that we kept in dispatch, which seemed way too astringent and strong for that purpose. But the odd behavior fit his tidy personality. He drank a lot of coffee and stepped quickly and purposefully. He smelled of cologne all day long.

He started many of his stories with "Riddle me this!" because there was always a point. There was always a question, and he was always poised to answer it.

If this is beginning to sound like a eulogy, that's because it *is* a eulogy.

As captain of the administrative and dispatch departments, Mack was highly protective of his direct reports. As a former street cop (but not directly in charge of the cops at White Bear), he was highly critical of those street cops, constantly second-guessing decisions they made in tough situations and comparing their methods to what he might have done as Mr. Perfect Street Cop in Port St. Lucie. As a result: we dispatchers loved him, while the cops frequently referred to him as "that fucking guy" or, when there was more than one possible fucking guy, "that *short* fucking guy."

But all the tough talk and puffery just seemed like family squabbling to me, still something of an outsider myself. When Tris, our weekend dispatcher, stalled her car on a hot day on the freeway, and Mack found out she hadn't called the PD for help, he about blew a gasket. "What are we here for if not to help each other?" he huffed. "She called some Joe Fucking Shmo instead of us? She knows better. She knows better!"

Rumors flew around about a shooting Mack had somehow botched in Port St. Lucie, in which a bystander had been killed. I never asked him. It seems to me that whenever anyone comes from a southern state to the land of seven-month winters, we in the north always suspect the worst. He must have done something bad. Because *why would anyone just move here?*

Anyway, when you work for a police department, all your sins are quite exhaustively evaluated before you join. I figured whatever happened in Port St. Lucie, if he'd passed the department sniff test, he was fine.

As I mine my memories about Mack, I find myself doing what I always do when I think about him. I'm trying to solve a mystery. A *riddle.* I'm trying to figure out what happened, or if it could have been stopped. I'm trying to paint a picture of my friend Mack, whose face I will never forget (and I've forgotten a lot), and I'm trying to make you like him, as much as anyone could like him. Because love him or hate him, White Bear Lake Police Captain J. W. Lyttle is gone forever.

∼

It was a quiet evening shift when I got a call on one of the non-emergent lines. I recognized the number right away as belonging to a neighboring county dispatch center. The dispatcher, a woman, asked for the police chief. I said she wasn't there but I could get a message to her.

"When would she get that?" the dispatcher wanted to know.

Soon.

Usually at that hour of night, the chief would have been long gone. But on this night, she was attending a swearing-in at the adjacent city-hall building.

"Can I ask what it's regarding?" I said, assuring her for a second time that the message would be delivered shortly.

"It's regarding a death."

About twenty minutes later, I started noticing a lot of movement. Someone had turned on the lights in the chief's office and in Mack's office. One of our detectives, a petite brown-haired lady named Amanda, had arrived and was milling around the records department. Three or four of our street cops had parked their squads and were speaking in hushed tones in the hallway between dispatch and the squad room.

Had Amanda been at city hall? Had she come in from home? Her girlish face was stern and her voice was low.

"I'm going to be calling a lot of people and leaving messages," she said. "Just direct them to me in here."

"Okay," I said, clueless. I wanted to ask, but felt paralyzed. Maybe I didn't want to know.

Amanda disappeared. Then another of our detectives appeared.

A 911 line lit up, a cell phone.

"911?"

"Hi, I want to report a drunk driver."

"Where is this?"

"Northbound on I-35 East. He's all over the road. Almost sideswiped me."

"Can you get a license plate?"

"I don't think so."

"Are you following?"

"I can't."

So much of this job is just relaying messages. It's a big, long, never-ending game of operator. You tell me this, and I take the information and I give it to someone who dispatches someone, who may or may not ever really get there in time. This one belonged to state patrol, so I hit their non-emergent line and proceeded to regurgitate.

By the tone in the dispatcher's voice, it didn't sound like any troopers were anywhere near this guy. Still, message sent and message received. I know all I need to know, and now so does she.

Regarding a death.

Amanda came buzzing back into the records room, and I couldn't take it anymore. I hustled close to the window of my little cage.

"What are people going to call me back about? What's going on?"

A temporary look of horror crossed her face.

"I thought you knew," she breathed. "You took the message."

"For the chief? They just said there was a death. That's all."

"Mack killed himself," she said apologetically. "I thought they told you. He shot himself at Mia's house."

It's hard to dispatch while crying, but it's not the first time I've done it. Mack would have been proud I didn't curl up in a ball in the bathroom, or just get in my car and start driving. I stayed and did my job. Like I had a choice? Like Mack asked any of us what we wanted? Of course, we all just kept working. He would have said that's the way they do it in Port St. Lucie. But that's the way they do it everywhere.

~

Mack's funeral was small. It's hard to know how to celebrate someone who takes himself out of the game so violently and so aggressively, as he did, with a gun, at the house he once shared with his girlfriend.

The chaplain who gave his eulogy seemed only to know that Mack was a tough man to know. He couched it with descriptors like "stubborn" and "perfectionist." I wanted to at least stand up and say, "You know, when Mack used to stand in dispatch for sometimes hours, pontificating about 'real police work' and 'riddle me this' and giggling like a kid about some stupid thing his basset hound did? I will miss that."

But I didn't stand up and say anything for Mack.

As some sort of tribute to Mack's warm-weather roots, or maybe the silly Hawaiian shirts he wore on Fridays, a Beach Boys song was played toward the end of the service. But it was an awkward attempt at levity that simply bounced off the church walls, past the uniformed officers who generally hated *that fucking guy*, and fell flat.

Truth is, I think we were all just really pissed off at him.

Even more so when the chief mandated us all to talk about our feelings.

About six months before Mack died, our department had also lost a female officer in about the same way. I knew very little about her death, except that Linda had been depressed, and she had kept her darkest feelings to herself. She had driven her personal vehicle to a remote area and shot herself.

Desperate to make sure nobody else on her department was going to do what Linda and Mack had done, our chief decided that each of us must talk to a grief counselor in the weeks after Mack's death. Without exception, all cops and dispatchers had to submit to therapy at least once.

That fucking guy.

The counselor, a middle-aged cop named Rodney, was an easy enough guy to talk to. He came to me in dispatch one afternoon, and we chatted on and off for several hours. Like me, he was a recovering alcoholic and regular at Alcoholics Anonymous. He was career law enforcement. He had once worked with my husband, and we knew a lot of the same people at Ramsey County. So of course when he asked me if I was having any thoughts of suicide, I looked him right in the eye—and lied.

In emergency services, we talk to crazy people all the time. That's how we tend to see them, not as depressed or troubled or trauma-tized. We put them in a box labeled "Crazy" so that their troubles won't begin to trouble *us*. *Crazy people* commit suicide. Crazy people line their homes with tinfoil or duct tape or Post-it notes. Crazy people call us and demand to talk to Jesus Christ. Or they believe they *are* Jesus Christ. Crazy people go to psych wards in hospitals, especially when they say they are thinking about suicide.

In the weeks since Mack's death, I had felt responsible somehow. There we were, Mack and I, spending hours and hours in dispatch, talking about dogs and vacations and all manner of inane bullshit, and all the while he hadn't known I was a recovering addict and I hadn't known he was suffering. It was a hugely egotistical notion to blame myself, but as a writer and an addict, I'm totally prone to all manner of magical thinking.

But I kept it to myself. And the defeated, suicidal feelings that accompanied that, I stuffed them way down. I certainly wasn't going to reveal them to a cop, sanctioned by my boss, the chief, so I could be put on a seventy-two-hour hold and sent to a hospital.

"Hey, doesn't Caroline work today?"

"No, she's on a three-day spin-dry down at county."

Hell, no.

I figured those feelings would pass. And they did pass. I'm not saying that I did the right thing; I'm just saying that's what I did at the time. I knew that keeping those feelings to myself made me no better than Mack or Linda. In some twisted way, it made what they did easier to forgive.

"911?"

"Hello, this is Don. Over on Hazel. You remember me?"

"Sure, Don. What do you need?"

"Well, I've got those voices again."

"Okay, what are they saying?"

"You know, the usual things. You know."

"Okay. I'll send someone over."

"Can you send that Jenny over again?"

"No, but the guys I'm sending are very nice. They'll talk to you."

"Okay. I guess that's okay."

7

Monkeys on Typewriters

The rules of emergency services scheduling are as follows:

1) Everybody hates their hours, except the most senior people, who get the choice daytime hours.

2) By the time the most senior people get the choice daytime hours they so richly deserve, they are either too bitter or too burned out to appreciate that they finally have the choice daytime hours. Also, their children are grown, basically negating the once-urgent need for choice daytime hours.

3) Colonies of humans will be living on Mars and cancer will have been cured long before any one person will ever draft a schedule that will make an entire staff of dispatchers happy.

4) If given an infinite timeframe, a monkey randomly hitting keys on a typewriter will eventually bang out a schedule that all dispatchers will equally *dislike*, and then that monkey will be hired as manager of said dispatch center—despite never having dispatched 911 a day in his little monkey life.

5) Some people actually choose night hours . . . and even prefer them to day hours. These people should not be trusted. Their character disorders range from anti-management stress knitters to outright sociopaths. They are not management material, but they are great fun at parties. And they are always the last to leave said parties because they have no idea it's 3:30 A.M.

5.5) Night shift is the worst.

6) Some people don't complain about their hours but just accept them as par for the course. I don't trust these people, either. They end up getting hired as trainers because they are so tolerant and patient, which ironically gets them the choice daytime hours the rest of us complainers want so badly.

7) If you are a big enough schedule complainer, sooner or later the union rep (usually a senior dispatcher who has been there long enough to get the choice daytime hours) will encourage you to take over as union rep. Never, *ever* fall for this. This is a dirty trick that will not only *not* get you better hours but will also require you to attend long arduous daytime meetings when you should be sleeping.

7.5) Schedules actually make us want to harm each other. Some people dream of being able to afford a bigger house, some dream of trading in their old Chevy sedans for new Saabs . . . dispatchers dream of seniority. We dream to the point where if one of our more tenured dispatchers has to have a surgery or perhaps gets into a car accident, someone might joke, "Hey, seniority, baby!" We don't actually wish for bad things to happen to the more senior people . . . well, actually, yes, we do. But on the lowest level possible for the better hours to come available and move the rest of us up the scheduling totem pole. That's all. Really.

8) There is one thing worse than night shift: the afternoon shift.

My shift at White Bear Lake PD was the worst. I hated the 2:00 P.M.–10:00 P.M. shift with a fiery, all-consuming, ridiculous passion. Also, it was a rotating shift, so I had no constant nights off. It was four on, two off. Four on, two off. So, for example, if I wanted to make my husband take a ballroom dance class with me, I couldn't; I never had the same night off from week to week. I never really wanted that, but knowing I couldn't have it made me not-want it less.

The hardest thing about working afternoons was trying to parent. During my first two years at Ramsey County, I was educated in all the bad things that kids can get into . . . in other cities. At White Bear Lake PD, I learned (astoundingly) that all these shenanigans were also taking place in the city in which Jim and I were trying to raise our daughter.

Methamphetamines, sex parties, joyrides, shoplifting, vandalism, binge drinking, date rape, runaways. As far as I could tell, this (plus a little bit of Xbox) was what *all the kids* were into. And I was terrified.

Between the hours of 2:00 P.M. and 10:00 P.M. each day, instead of making sure my daughter was not participating in any of the aforementioned shenanigans, I was listening to other parents' tales of after-school woe.

"My daughter just got home from school late, and she's been drinking Listerine."

"My son just stole my car!"

"My daughter has been missing since Tuesday."

When she was twelve, Mariah joined a softball team. Softball was a childhood obsession of mine, and I wanted to be at every game screaming my lungs out, berating the high-school-aged umpires, and indulging in ice cream afterward like a good mom, but I almost never could because of my schedule.

"Can we switch for my daughter's softball game on Wednesday?" I'd sometimes ask Janet, the most senior dispatcher, who of course had the choice daytime hours.

"I sure wish I could," she'd say earnestly, and I could almost forgive the lie because if our positions were reversed, I wouldn't have been so diplomatic. Why should she switch? She'd been there something like twenty years to my five months. Suck it up, newbie.

That summer, I got to only three out of fifteen softball games.

But when I wasn't bellyaching about my hours at work . . . I was actually kind of having fun.

"911?"

"Hi. I'm in my car and I'm following my girlfriend, and she has my cell phone, and I want you to send someone to pull her over."

"Whose phone do you have right now?"

"You need to get someone over here! She's on County Road F in a green Grand Prix!"

"And you are following her right now?"

"Yes!"

"And you have someone else's cell phone?"

"Yes! You need to send someone right now!"

"I'm not going to send someone to pull your girlfriend over, but if you will pull over, I'll send an officer to talk to you about it."

"That's bullshit! She stole my phone!"

"I'm sorry, but that's actually a civil issue between you and your girlfriend. I'd be happy to . . ."

"Listen, you fucking idiot—"

"Did you just call me an idiot?" Not sure why I needed clarification on that. I heard him loud and clear. But I have to say—I was a bit surprised.

"Yeah! How would you like it if I came down and bombed your fucking police department?"

I would *not* like that sir. Yet, I *do* like that you just said that because . . . *felony terroristic threats. It's a thing.* He could call me a fucking idiot all day long, and the most he'd get is a lecture from a well-meaning officer. But threatening to bomb the police department on a recorded line shows a felony-level lack of decorum.

"I'd really like you to pull over, *sir.* I can send someone who can help you with this issue with your girlfriend."

"Are they going to get my phone back?"

"Where are you again?"

"I'm at White Bear and Cedar, but she's getting away!"

"What's your last name, *sir?*"

"It's Chatham."

"What are you driving?"

Eventually, I convinced my young caller to pull over. We had his name, so arresting him on the spot wasn't urgent or entirely necessary, but I just super duper wanted him to get arrested *on my shift.*

"Did you just call me an idiot?" I said again, this time on the recording as Amanda and I listened to it in dispatch.

"No, he called you a *'fucking idiot,'*" she giggled.

"Right," I said, smiling wryly. "What's going to happen to him?"

"We're going to see if he's the same guy calling in these other bomb threats we were getting. But he's in enough trouble with just this."

"Nail 'im to the wall!" I exclaimed.

"Aww. Is this your first time being called a fucking idiot?"

"Directly to me, yes! It's just so . . . *rude.*"

"You get used to it."

About six months later, I got a summary of Mr. Chatham's court appearance. Along with his time in the workhouse, his sentence included writing a letter of apology to me personally. I never saw that letter. I wouldn't have bought it anyway.

"How did your game go, sweetie?" I asked Mariah at the end of that shift.

"We lost."

"I'm sorry. Did everybody look cute in their pink tube socks?"

"Yeah! We got our matching visors tonight, too!"

"I'm sorry I missed that."

"It's okay. Can you make the next one?"

"If Janet switches with me, sure!"

"Does she ever switch with you?"

"Yes . . . well . . . no. But I think I'm wearing her down."

"When can you start working the day shift?"

"When you're in college, most likely."

"That sucks."

I don't like it when she says "sucks" because it's almost a curse word. And cursing leads to hanging out with bad kids, which leads to skipping school, which leads to . . . methamphetamines and running away with stolen cars and date rapists!

All between the hours of 2:00 P.M. and 10:00 P.M.

"Yeah," I sigh. "It really kind of sucks."

"911?"

"Yeah, I need you to send someone right now. My kid is out of control."

"Is that him screaming in the background?"

"Yeah. I took his Xbox away, and I'm trying to get him to go to school. I need someone to come over here and make him go to school."

"We can't make him go to school either. Is he violent?"

"Will that get you to come over?"

"Ma'am. Is he violent?"

"He threatened me, if that's what you mean."

"Does he have any weapons?"

"Just in his little fantasyland videogames."

"Okay, we'll be over shortly."

8

Cops

When a stranger at a party learns that I'm a dispatcher, he or she often takes that special opportunity to tell me how much he or she dislikes the police.

"I got pulled over on Arcade *for nothing*. Cops are assholes."

"I got a parking ticket, and I wasn't even there three minutes!"

"I got a DWI, but I'd only had two beers."

(Just an aside: Everybody in the history of driving while intoxicated has only had two beers. Independent research by DWI suspects all over the country suggests that any blood-alcohol reading from .2 to brain-dead can be achieved with only two beers. There ought to be public service announcements in which earnest and concerned celebrities give this solemn warning: "Friends don't let friends drink *two beers*.")

Anyway, I never know what to say to those people. Except, maybe, "It's complicated." But that sounds condescending. Which makes me sound like a cop. Now there is a risk that my new acquaintance will walk away thinking, "Wow. Dispatchers are assholes."

"Dispatch, I need you to confirm a stolen for me. I'm eastbound White Bear Avenue at South Shore."

"Copy, 332. Stand by."

"Copy. *Standing by.*"

He's—very subtly—being an asshole. He wants to do his job and pull this guy over, but he needs more information. But I can't get it *right this second* because, as usual, I'm already ass-deep in alligators, and it involves me making a phone call to the county. It's a fairly routine stop, and he could be nice, or he could give me attitude.

A couple of months ago, I was surfing the web for local news and noticed this headline: "Mendota Heights officer shot . . ." And I thought I had lost a friend.

To work with cops is to live with the knowledge that one moment I could be sharing a coffee with a coworker and telling him all about my new rescue dog or my daughter's first car, and then hours later, he could get into a squad car, ride off, and be gone forever. It could happen any time. My husband, also a dispatcher, once got the news of a fallen coworker by hearing it on a public radio news report. When a second coworker of his was killed months later, I intercepted the news on Facebook and made sure he heard it from me instead.

It had been several years since Cheryl and I had worked together as dispatchers or even met for a coffee, but I knew that she was a Mendota Heights officer. Was she the one? Was she the *Mendota Heights officer shot*? I pictured her three daughters' faces as I scoured the news stories for names, or even the telltale pronoun *she*. Nothing. I finally texted a mutual friend, who mercifully responded promptly. "It's not her," she wrote. "It's a guy. He has a wife and kids."

Equal parts relief and shame washed over me. Relief that Cheryl was alive. Shame that my joy in that fact meant that some other family, some other friends, would not be spared from losing the police officer that *they* loved.

It happened during a "routine" traffic stop. Officer Scott Patrick had pulled over a man in a vehicle and was shot in the face.

"There's no such thing as a routine traffic stop," we hear a lot in this business. Unfortunately, that's not exactly true. There are a lot of stops that look the same. They're harmless, meaningless, and *routine.* And cops and dispatchers can get comfortable. And then somebody gets shot in the face.

At last I make that phone call and learn that 332's traffic stop is actually *not routine.*

"332, that's a confirmed stolen."

"Copy. I'll be stopping him at 61 and 7th."

And then what?

"344. I'm en route to 332's stop."

"Copy, 344. You're en route to 61 and 7th."

But she is at least two minutes away. What will happen for that first two minutes? We are well beyond the days of saying, "Oh, that never happens."

Maybe that's the kind of thing that makes humans into assholes. The fear. Or if not the fear, then the stress from stuffing the fear way down. *I'll be stopping this guy, who possibly stole this vehicle, and he might not want to be stopped, and I sure do hope he's not pissed off enough about that to assault me, or shoot me in the face.*

"I'm anti-cop," some guy said to me once. At a party. You'd think I'd learn to stop attending social events.

What to even say to that? Where to go from there?

"Hell, yeah! I'm anti-cop, too. We need to starting arming kittens with airsoft guns and training them in conflict negotiation and verbal judo. Right on, man. Human law enforcement *is so last century.*"

But it was one year after the now-infamous shooting in Ferguson. He was angry about Ferguson and confused about so many videos he'd seen and news clips he'd read since that time, about innocent, unarmed black Americans being shot and killed by police.

So it doesn't do it anymore to say, "They're not *all* like that." Because we all know that. Even those of us who support the kitten militia. That's not the issue. The issue is bigger than the little town I dispatch in, and bigger than the handful of cops I know, and bigger than whether one cop is racist or one cop is not.

Sometimes, I wish the good cops would just work harder to be nicer, to make up for the bad ones. Many of them do, but it's not something you'll see on CNN. Instead, we see them at protests and demonstrations with automatic weapons and riot gear. And these cops stop having faces, and they all just look frightening as hell.

"I'm not anti-cop," I stuttered eventually to the man at the party, feeling like a complete Judas, both to all of the victims of bad cops and to all of the good cops I adore so much. It's just not that simple for me. I can't be objective. I can't be a person who sends them on these errands, these awful dangerous and foolhardy errands that nobody else wants to go on, and then betrays them at parties. No matter what video has gone viral, no matter what tragic or cruel thing any given officer has done, I can't put them all in a basket and label it "Assholes."

What I really wanted was to tell him the peanut butter–toast story. Because whenever someone tells me that cops are assholes, I think about peanut butter toast.

Officer Gunderson (Brenna) once showed up on a cardiac-arrest call and found that she was first on the scene. The elderly patient needed chest compressions plus rescue breathing. At one point during the rescue breaths, the patient vomited into Brenna's mouth. It was peanut butter toast.

"I'll never eat peanut butter toast again!" she said merrily, on her way to another medical, where she might be called on to do something equally awful.

Ten years later, when I asked her about the peanut butter story, she just shrugged.

"Peanut butter toast, huh? I mean, I'm sure that happened," she said nodding briskly. There have been so many more peanut butter–esque scenes for her since then. Too many to recall.

I don't tell the peanut butter story at parties. If Gunderson doesn't use it for sympathy, then I sure as hell can't. She now works as a police liaison at the high school, where she could be called upon at any moment to administer rescue breaths to kids with braces and mystery meat in their mouths. Or she could just encounter an active shooter and be required, in that moment, to sacrifice her own life for those kids. For about two bucks more an hour than what I make. I'll take the pay cut.

Anyway, cops are assholes.

That's what people tell me, anyway.

"Uh . . . 322 to 300?"

"322, go ahead."

"The north rig will be going en route shortly with mom to Regions."

"Copy . . ."

"And I'll be out with five all under the age of seven. We'll be . . . uh . . . playing with Barbies until Grandma gets on scene."

"Copy. Barbies. Is the . . . scene secure?"

"Ah . . . affirm. For now."

"10:52."

9

Missing

"WhiteBearLakePoliceandFire?"

"Hello. Yes. I want to report that I think I saw that young man who went missing. You know? The West Point one?"

"Okay, where did you see him, ma'am?"

"I was at the Maplewood Mall, coming out of Sears, and there he was."

"What was he doing?"

"He was just walking. He had a Hollister bag."

Mitch Rinken went missing in December 2006, just before Christmas.

People go missing a lot. Parents often call to report their teenagers "missing," but cops don't often jump. Instead, they file some paperwork, make sure there's nothing suspicious going on, and wait. It doesn't make it to the evening news. We don't see their pictures. When adults are reported missing, it's often because they just don't want to be found. There's been a fight, or a falling out, or a mess that can't be cleaned up. There's nothing fishy about that, only sad.

But twenty-one-year-old Mitch Rinken was different. He was a freshman cadet who had come home from West Point for Christmas break, not a typical *missing*. He had also driven drunk with some friends, crashed his mother's car, and had some understandably uncomfortable exchanges with his parents one day before he disappeared. So, it *was* fishy. At least, a little bit. And it sure made for a good news story. All the local networks were on it, and because of the West Point angle, it was even getting national coverage.

His picture was everywhere.

Anyone who thought they saw him was asked to call our non-emergent line, which of course was answered in our one-person dispatch center. His face was featured in newscast after newscast. The newsies seemed to really like the photo of him in his West Point uniform, with its stiff blue blazer and gold-toned buttons. His hair was more tousled than you would expect for a military school photo, and his smiling mouth seemed almost to be making a joke in the moment the photo was being taken.

"Are you going to send somebody?"

"When did you see him?"

"A couple of hours ago. I had some errands to run first, and then I came home."

"I'm going to pass your information along to the detectives, okay?"

"When?"

"Very soon." *Sooner than a couple of hours.*

Rinken had left his parents' White Bear Lake home sometime between 2:30 and 5:00 A.M., and nobody knew why, and nobody knew in what direction. But everybody was seeing the blond-haired, blue-eyed, all-American kid *everywhere.*

Mitch Rinken's parents and our police chief had recently been interviewed on a national news station, so the sightings were bound to keep rolling in for at least the next few days.

When I was seventeen, I went missing. But I was no Mitch Rinken. When I went missing, I was a runaway with a drug habit and an older boyfriend. Since it was only weeks before my eighteenth birthday, police filed the information but did nothing with it. Nobody suspected anything fishy. No reason to. Just another teenage rebellion.

About four days after leaving the state, I did finally call my parents to let them know I was alive, and probably to see if they would send me money. I was in Cleveland for that first call. My mom once lived in Cleveland and never had a lot of nice things to say about it. She cried. She wouldn't send me money, but said she was glad that I was okay and that she loved me.

Several months later, I returned to my parents with lots of apologies and the promise to enter drug treatment. While staying at their house, I came across a photo of them that had been taken on my dad's birthday not long after I'd left the state with my boyfriend. They must have been told to smile, and maybe they thought they were smiling, but mostly they just looked like they were keeping each other from sliding off a cliff. I thought of that photo every time I saw the Rinkens.

"White Bear Lake Police and Fire. How may I help you?"

"You know that Rinken kid?"

"The young man who is missing?"

"Yeah. I'm pretty sure I saw him hitchhiking in Wisconsin. You know? Just over the border."

"Okay, let me get some information from you . . ."

Young Mitch smiled at me as if he had just told me something funny. I could not smile back. *Kid, if you are in fact walking around with a Hollister bag in a mall somewhere, or if you're hitchhiking to Cleveland, and you haven't called those poor people, then you're the biggest jerk to ever leave White Bear Lake.*

No, wait. *That would be me.* But as big a jerk as I was, I called. That's how I knew Mitch Rinken wasn't walking around—anywhere. I suspect his parents knew that, too.

Of the dozens of names I'd entered into the national database as "missing," Mitch Rinken's photo was one of just a few I'd seen. Many didn't have photos on file, or if they did, they weren't smiling. I wondered what the others looked like. I wondered what their parents looked like. I wondered if any of these people were ever going to see each other again, and why the world seemed to care about only one of them.

After a few weeks, the Rinken sightings tapered off, the reporters found new things to write about, and time went on for everyone except the Rinkens, I imagine. Winter turned to spring, and Mitch Rinken didn't come home, and he didn't call.

Mitch's body was found on a melty spring day in April 2007 in Goose Lake, at the western border of the city. Police ruled his death an accidental drowning. He was wearing running clothes and was less than three miles from his parents' house. There was nothing fishy about it, only sad.

"911?"

"Okay. Do you have a minute?"

"Um. There's really no way to know."

10

Tell Me Exactly
What Happened

When I first started at WBPD, I was required to take a three-day course to become a certified "emergency medical dispatcher." An EMD is a dispatcher who uses a predetermined set of questions to find out just what is wrong with the patient, whether to send help routinely or emergent, and then gives pre-arrival instructions to follow while help is on the way.

I freaking loved it. Here it was: the script I'd been asking for my whole career.

As EMDs, we were given a set of alphabetized and laminated cards with all manner of malady and calamity and trained how to use them. We merely had to flip to the right card to find a list of all the right questions to ask.

Oh, you're having chest pain? Let me just flip to the "chest pain" card. You have a patient trapped in a vehicle? Let me just flip to the "extrication" card. You have pneumonia? Sick card. What's that you say? *Ammonia?* Inhalation card!

It was a Caroline-proof system.

And depending on how the caller answered, the solutions were in the cards, too.

The patient's not breathing? Here's how you start chest compressions!

The patient's choking? Let me tell you how to do the Heimlich!

We were taught strict adherence to the scripts. If you stick to the script, we were told, you will do fine. No freelancing. The EMD greeting went like this: After gathering the initial address, callback number, and name, we were to ask: "What's the problem, tell me exactly what happened." Cheesy and cumbersome, yes. I did not care. (Grammatically incorrect. That messed with me a little.)

My only sadness was that the cards only covered medical emergencies. I wanted cards for everything. Armed robberies? Jurisdictional clusterfucks? Missing loved ones? Troubling teenagers? *Let me just find the card real quick . . .*

I returned from training all revved up on the idea of scripted dispatching. I felt supported. I felt ready. I felt *like I knew stuff.*

"I never use the things," the night dispatcher, Victoria, told me on my first evening back after the training. Sure enough, there sat the cards well out of her reach on a counter by the records window.

"Why not?"

"I don't have time," she shrugged.

"But you could get someone started on CPR! You could save a life!"

Her mouth said, "Well . . . that's . . ." but her eyes said, *"Newbie."*

"You'll find out."

And I did.

"911?"

"Help me, help! I just found my husband in the bathroom and he's not breathing!"

"Are you at 5614 Lakeridge Road?"

"Yes!"

"Okay, hold on."

Now comes paging the members of the volunteer fire department, listening for them to answer one at a time, then answering them—one at a time. That's small-town dispatching, and it's never fast—it's cheesy and cumbersome.

Long tones sound (beeeeeeep boooooooop). "North end ALS for a fifty-seven-year-old male unconscious and not breathing at 5614 Lakeridge

Road." *Beeeeeep booooop.* Second verse, same as the first: "Need a north end ALS for a fifty-seven-year-old male uncon and not breathing at 5614 Lakeridge Road. 14:35."

Now they start calling in.

"452 EMT en route to the station."

"Copy, 14:35."

"430 medic en route to the scene."

"430 copied."

"415, here. Was that Lakeridge Road?" Yes, twice.

"Affirm, 415."

"Copy. En route to the station to pick up the . . ."

Argh. Too much talk. Cops are trained to be succinct and paid to be professional. Volunteer firefighters are trained to come in when they can, and they are not paid. And if I don't like how slowly they talk, I can pound sand. Because they are not paid. And I don't remember the last time I volunteered—for anything—unpaid.

After two or three full minutes, I can finally get back to my caller, who is now in near hysterics because I've left her alone with her not-breathing husband for what seems like an hour. She's dropped the phone and is yelling at him to wake up.

"What's the problem, tell me exactly what's . . . ma'am are you there? Ma'am?"

It's great to have the training, and the cards are a nice security blanket. And like Victoria, I almost *never used them.* But I wanted to. Why should the cops and firefighters get to save everybody?

And then deeper than my grandiose superhero lifesaving fantasies lived a terrible fear: that if I wasn't able to give those lifesaving instructions, someone could die as a result, and I would be culpable. It would be my voice on some awful recording attached to an untimely death. On the ten-o'clock news. "Listen as the mother of a one-month-old begs for CPR instructions, and the 911 dispatcher puts her on hold!"

Who would it be? A baby? A neighbor? Whose life was going to slip past me while I was busy with other things?

You're being dramatic, I was told. *We've never had a problem.*

Hard logic to argue with, and true.

It's how we've always done it.

You could almost hear Tevye from *Fiddler on the Roof* every time I brought it up. ("Tradition!")

Anyone who's ever worked or lived in a small town knows how much the locals *love it* when a newbie comes in and tells them they're doing *everything wrong*. So my concerns about the one-person system fell on deaf ears all the way up and down the chain of command.

What I proposed was that WBPD contract with an ambulance service so that instead of putting callers on hold, we could transfer them to a secondary answering service of EMDs that could give instructions.

Then one day it occurred to me: wouldn't it be fun to be one of those EMDs? And then—*ding!* A light went on.

Caller: "Okay, honey. I think the officer is here. I'd better let you go so I can put my teeth in."

II

Starting Over

The Ambulance Company (not its real name) is my third dispatch center. It is the third place where I have agreed to start at the bottom of the seniority totem pole. The third set of policies, the third pile of maps, the third new way of doing everything.

Here, I will only be dispatching medical emergencies as an EMD. I will be *Little Miss Pre-arrival*. And, oh hell yes—I will save lives.

Tell me exactly what happened—so I can fix it! *Boom.*

The Ambulance Company (let's call it TAC) is considered a "secondary" answering point. All calls transferred to us have first been answered by a county or city 911 center. This is so lovely. It means that someone else has had to ascertain an address and a problem. It means no dog-barking complaints. It means no missing cell phones. No foot chases, no chasing down drunk drivers. Just medicals, 24-7.

Calls come "prepackaged," which makes them sound like food or personal items to me. But what it means is that the primary dispatcher (usually) introduces the call with a predictable little packet of info: "This is Blah County. We have a seventy-six-year-old male with chest pain at 123 ABC Street. Buzz the security door to get in. I have his wife, Joni, on the phone."

Neat and clean, *right?*

Before accepting the job, I get a chance to sit with one of the EMDs for a couple of hours. I hold back my guffaw when she tells me she's dispatched there for thirty-three years. Back when it was the "switchboard."

Ruth seems happy enough. It's rare to meet a *jubilant* dispatcher, I've learned by this point. ("When I grow up, I want to be the unfortunate middle person who must relay vital information between thousands of people having their worst days ever, and the sometimes bitter and burned-out cops and paramedics who have to help them!" said no child, ever.)

As we chat, a new call flashes onto the screen in front of her. With barely a pause, she selects the closest ambulance from the seven rigs available.

"711, take a code 3 for one with a severe nosebleed," she says casually, waits for the ambulance crew to answer. She announces the address, assigns the call to 711 in the CAD (computer-aided dispatch system), then turns back to me.

"How do you like it?"

"It's all right, you know."

"How is the staffing?"

"Well, it could be better."

"When you have to go to the bathroom, do you generally . . . get to go? Without an issue?"

Ruth pauses, drums her fingers on the console.

"Yeah," she says finally. "Most of the time."

Sold.

It crosses my mind that if you take away all the domestics, the chases, the pets on the loose, the traffic stops . . . I could get bored. But mainly I'm here for two things: freedom to give good and thorough pre-arrival instructions, and freedom to pee when I need to. And maybe I could use a little boredom.

The schedule is a bit better, mostly because I'm working part time instead of full time.

I measure my success in summer softball games. That summer, I make it to so many of Mariah's games that one day she says, "You know, don't feel like you have to go to *all* of them."

She is sick of me! A parenting win.

DISPATCHER: "Ma'am, did you hurt anything other than your ankle when you fell?"

ELDERLY FEMALE CALLER: "Just my pride and my ass."

12

My People

My favorite thing about TAC: I have people again! Not that cops and firefighters aren't people, but they aren't *my people*. People who know what it's like to bounce back and forth from two or three 911 lines, *while* paging the fire department, *while* checking the status of an out-of-state driver's license, *while* trying to finish chewing a bite of turkey sandwich—those people are my people.

During a shift at TAC, some of us function mainly as call-takers, fielding calls and giving pre-arrival instructions, and some of us function mainly as dispatchers, assigning calls to ground ambulance and medical helicopter crews. But *all* are trained to dispatch and call-take for all of the regions that TAC serves, and all are charged with *backing each other up*.

The first of my trainers is also the supervisor of the dispatch center, the handsome and impeccably styled and appropriate Luke M. (Picture the supervisor from *Office Space*, only funny and likable.) I arrive early on my first day, and he is ready for me in a conference room with a policy manual the size of *Watership Down*. He takes out a small personal thermos and begins to pour himself a cup, then stops abruptly.

"I should ask,"—genuine concern furrows his brows—"do you mind the smell of coffee?"

"Huh?"

"The smell, it doesn't bother you?"

"Who doesn't like the smell of coffee? What *dispatcher* doesn't like the smell of coffee?"

Luke laughs. "Wait till you get the list."

"The list?"

"Yeeeeaaahhh," he shrugs. "We have some particular people around here. *Anyway* . . . uh . . . we have a few policy items to go over."

He flips to page one of the three-inch binder.

"The thing about dispatching for so many different cities and counties," he says apologetically, "is that they all have their own way of doing things. And they all tend to be . . . different from each other."

Hence, three inches of policy.

"Don't worry," he smiles. "You get used to it." This, I've heard before.

Good thing we both like the smell of coffee.

~

My new employer is actually a medical transportation service, a private company, not a public entity. But our ambulance services are contracted by cities and counties all over the state who, if they don't like our services, can look around for someone else. So we basically work for everybody. And you know what they say about pleasing *everybody*.

Some towns and townships are so sparsely populated that the closest ambulance is still twenty to thirty minutes away, assuming that ambulance is at its post and not on another call. If that one ambulance gets a call, we dispatchers then need to figure out "coverage." We do this by moving an ambulance from another town halfway or all the way to the town that just lost coverage, depending on how many trucks there are in the larger area.

Areas with sparse coverage depend heavily on local "first responders" who live in the area and often have to use their personal vehicles to respond to the calls, but who can be on the scene within five or ten minutes of the call going out. These folks have little in the way of equipment, and they know their "backup" (ambulance) is still several minutes away. Fifteen minutes. Half an hour. And with nothing but love and respect for those brave people, I will never, *ever* live in an area that depends heavily on first responders. I'm way too paranoid. Want to know where the nearest trauma center is? Heart hospital? Both? I can tell you. I'm rarely more than five minutes away from either. Why? I am perfectly healthy. And—because of this job— royally paranoid.

I overhear my cohorts refer to our coverage duties as a constant "game of chess"—because we are moving trucks like chess pieces all over the map. But frankly, I grew up playing chess with my grandpa, and chess, to me, is a peaceful game of contemplation peppered with conversation and long sips of lemonade. The game of chess would only compare to coverage if the rules changed by e-mail from management roughly every other move, and if the pawns were always trying to move themselves. And if all of this was taking place at gunpoint. Then maybe.

"732, if you could head to 32nd [Avenue] for coverage."

(We say *if you could* a lot when what we really mean is *now you will. Five minutes ago. Chop-chop.*)

"Uh, dispatch, it's after 10:00 P.M."

And that's . . . your bedtime?

"We don't use that post after ten," my trainer advises me. Wade Wilson is one of my many trainers, and he's trying really hard not to let me get my ass kicked by the metro night-shift medics. And that's—really difficult.

"Copy, 732." I scour the complex metro coverage chart in order to figure out where they *should* be if not 32nd.

I run through the pertinent coverage questions. Where are the holes that need to be filled? Where is this truck needed? How quickly can they fill the hole based on where they are now? Is there a truck close to its end of shift? Should I fill that hole? Is there a truck at another hospital that is going to be clear soon? Is Highway 169 still closed? Is a new truck coming into service soon?

"Dispatch, we're at the tunnel." That's code for *make up your mind, newbie. Which exit? You've got about ten seconds.*

The other thing that's not at all like chess, the way I played it? Time limits. My grandpa used to take *days* contemplating his next move. He would not have liked the game of coverage. Not one bit.

"Station Two," Wade mumbles into his hand.

"Station Two!" I announce happily.

"Copy. Uh, can we swing up to quarters first? My partner forgot his lunch."

"No," Wade says.

"Affirm," I tell 732 at that exact moment.

"Really, dude? I'm trying to make friends, here."

"Sorry. No friends in dispatching."

"732, we need you at Two for now."

Long pause.

"Copy."

Wade squints at the map like we're not done moving trucks around. I so want to be done moving trucks around.

"And 722 should head to Station Four now."

"Shit. That's right. I had them en route to Two," I sigh.

"Yep. But now they can go back to Four."

"722, you can head back to Four."

"Copied, 700. *Turning around.*"

It's the weirdest thing. Paramedics *hate* turning around. As far as I know, their vehicles are 100 percent turnaround-capable, complete with steering wheels, tires, turn signals, and all the latest turning-around technology. Still. It's a thing with them.

"Copy. You're . . . turning around."

The game of coverage is very important. Failing at the game of coverage can mean adding several minutes to an ambulance crew's response time. It's also a guessing game. While I'm learning, Wade advises me to stick very closely to the coverage chart. But as a bit of an old-timer, he no longer needs to look at a chart, which fairly blows my mind. He advises me that it's a combination of having the chart memorized, sprinkled with a heavy helping of past experience and a dash of instinct.

Somewhere along the line, the term *Wilson coverage* was coined to describe any type of *nontraditional, off-the-chart* coverage.

Someone walking into the middle of a Wilson coverage situation may be heard to say, "So, *what have we got going on here?*"

It's a lot like grammar. You can break the rules of grammar or the rules of coverage eventually, but only once you know the rules. It got to where Wade didn't really like hearing the term "Wilson coverage" used all the time because it gave people the wrong impression, like he was going rogue all over the place with his coverage, or worse, that just anyone could imitate Wilson coverage.

It must not have been that bad an impression, as Wade eventually got promoted to supervisor. Though he left the dispatch trenches, the term *Wilson coverage* lived on. I guess *Wilson scheduling* just doesn't really roll off the tongue.

"Tell me exactly what happened."

"This guy just started having a seizure. My buddy is trying to put a fork in his mouth so he doesn't swallow his tongue."

"Tell him to stop that, right now. Don't put *anything* in his mouth."

"But I think I saw a movie once . . ."

"You can't swallow your tongue. No. Nothing in the mouth. Especially a fork."

"What about just his hand?"

"Not if he wants to keep his hand. I don't know what movie that's in, but *goodness, no.*"

13

Guns in the House

"This is Moore County with a transfer on a three-year-old who has been shot in the head by his brother."

I don't remember much of what I said after that, but I did talk a lot. I had to. In the area of this call, the closest ambulance and paramedic crew is usually fifteen to thirty minutes away, or more.

I'm sure my partner started both a ground ambulance and an air ambulance immediately, and I'm sure the police and fire departments were sent, too. But for several minutes, it was just me and this mother, and whatever terrible something she was seeing. What she was able to tell me let me know her son was probably beyond help.

"Hold him very still," I think I said.

She told me he appeared to still be breathing. This gave us both some false hope for a minute.

"Let's try to control the bleeding," I think I said.

"I don't think I can" was her reply.

I tried to keep her busy, and away from going into shock.

"Where is the gun?"

"Is your door unlocked?"

"Confirm your address for me?"

Rearranging chairs on her little sinking ship.

At some point, my mind briefly drifted to my own two young nephews, both close to that age. I think about the way a gunshot wound could explode a tiny head. I'm imagining any of it, all of it. What must she be seeing? How can she even speak?

Stop. Don't.

"They're coming as fast as they can," I tell her. That's the only thing I know for sure, so I say it many, many times. Probably ten or twenty cops, medics, and EMTs will be there soon, most of them parents, and they will have to see what has happened, and they will feel twice as helpless as I do.

The minutes tick by like little eternities.

There is a pre-arrival card for this, but there's not. When you run out of questions and answers, sometimes all you can do is just wait.

At long last, the first responders start arriving. I will learn later that the shooter was six years old. A terrible accident. The victim loved horseback riding and cars, a newspaper article said. His father couldn't be reached for comment about the *four* unsecured guns in the house.

This is not my first shooting call, but it is my first involving a child, committed by a child. This job is just chock-full of firsts you could never imagine.

Sometime after my first shooting call, I attempted to familiarize myself with gunshot wounds. What do they look like? What happens? Shouldn't I know? How can I send the rest of the world to these calls if I can't look upon the ugliness myself? Long story short, don't *ever* Google "gunshot wounds." And now you're going to because you're human. But don't say I didn't warn you.

"Are you going to the debriefing?" June asks me later. A debriefing is a meeting for all responders who were involved with a difficult call. It's a chance to talk about what happened, get other responders' takes on it. Process it. Learn from it. I could definitely use some processing, but the debriefing is two hours away, so I opt out. It seems frivolous to take that kind of time for myself when I'd only spent fifteen minutes on the phone. Whatever I was feeling paled in comparison to those who had to see the little boy, right? That's what I told myself, even though I'd never say those words to another dispatcher in that position. If it were another dispatcher, I'd have said, "You belong there just as much as anyone else."

DISPATCHER: "Do you have any pets that need to be put away before the medics get there?"

ELDERLY MALE CALLER: "Nope, I'm her only pet."

14

Doctor Phil Can Kiss My Hot Seat

Mariah is with me in the kitchen when the phone rings. The caller ID says "Paramount," which makes us both think it's someone looking for my husband, who, while also working as a 911 dispatcher, is a freelance screenwriter. This could be a big break, I figure, until I realize that it's for me.

"Ms. Burau? This is Jen from the *Dr. Phil Show*. I got your number from Mary at Borealis. Do you have time to talk?"

I wonder what kind of person doesn't have time to talk to *Jen from the Dr. Phil Show*. Probably nobody I've ever met, talked to, or even bumped up against in an airport bathroom.

"Yes. Sure! I'm free. I can certainly talk. Right now." I'm overselling, and I don't even know what she wants yet.

If Jen tells me at this point how she came to find my book, my brain is spinning too fast to even hear it. I wind down just enough to comprehend that she wants to fly me out to Los Angeles, that she's coordinating a show about 911 dispatch, and that this will all happen in about a week, if that works for me.

I utter any number of agreeable words and syllables, to the point where she's either realized what a small-time hick I am, or she's really marveling about the whole "Minnesota Nice" phenomenon. She promises to call in a couple of days with more details, and when we disconnect, I realize I've never once seen an episode of the *Dr. Phil Show*.

Despite my highest hopes, my flight to Phil is booked for the nose-bleed section. As I make my way through first class toward coach, I am in the same state I've been in all week, which is to say a state of cloudy, nervous happiness. I'm like an ant who has found a trail of syrup on the sidewalk, and who has decided this can only mean that a plate of perfect pancakes awaits at trail's end, and who, if he had a brain in his little ant head, would know that it likely only leads to a dumpster full of eggshells, bacon fat, and an empty Aunt Jemima bottle.

At first, I don't recognize her. Melissa Gilbert (of *Little House on the Prairie*) is red-haired and petite and has the otherworldly look of an aging actress who has had a little bit (but not a lot) of facial reconstruction. If I'm wrong about the plastic surgery, I apologize. But at the very least, some aggressive *tucking, waxing,* or *peeling* has taken place. But it's still her. It's Half-Pint.

And I'm staring. And then she lifts her head. And then *she's* staring back, but not in a way that says, "Hey, isn't that Caroline Burau, author of *Answering 911: Life in the Hot Seat* as seen on the *Dr. Phil Show?*"

Rather, Melissa Gilbert stares at me in a way that says, "Take a picture, it'll last longer. Freak." My first brush with fame, and I'm not even off the ground in Minneapolis. Snap! I brush past Melissa Gilbert's first-class hairdo and find my seat in coach, where I have a clear shot at the back of her head, just in case I haven't done enough staring yet.

My seatmate is a short blonde with a bobbed haircut and a Macintosh laptop. Her name is Alicia. She's divorced, she's got a teenage girl, she lives in Simi Valley, and, oh yeah, she's got tickets to sit in the audience at the *Dr. Phil Show* tomorrow. The same show I'll be at. We both guffaw at the coincidence for a minute; we're both going to Dr. Phil! As we talk, I gesture toward Melissa Gilbert's head.

"Did you see who's in first class?"

She had not. As we admire Melissa Gilbert's hair, I notice that the lady behind her is reading a book "authored" by none other than Robin McGraw, Dr. Phil's better half, who apparently comes to every single taping of his show and has become a pseudo-pseudo-celeb in her own housewife Barbie sort of way. Mrs. McGraw smiles at us from the cover of her book, which is meant to improve our lives with clever advice, with a smile that says: "Caroline. You are living in a Dr. Phil universe. It's time you knew."

All my life, I've never seen a single show. Now I'm traveling four hundred miles an hour toward Dr. Phil like livestock being dropped from the sky. I quote Mr. Carlson of *WKRP in Cincinnati*: "As God is my witness, I thought that turkeys could fly."

We disembark in L.A., and Alicia tells me she'll say a prayer for me to have a good show. I'll have one friend in the audience, and that's a comfort.

～

Dickipedia—yes, it's a real website—has this to say about Dr. Phil McGraw:

Sanctioned by the Texas State Board in 1989 for an "inappropriate relationship" with a 19-year-old patient, Dr. Phil was stripped of his license to practice psychology. To date, Dr. Phil has not completed the conditions required to regain his license, and remains unlicensed to practice psychology. Anywhere.

In my Hollywood Boulevard hotel room (how cool does that sound?!), I am checking my e-mail and waiting for room service to bring me my dinner ($50 voucher compliments of Phil): salmon and steamed veggies. My best friend Marie has sent me this link about Phil. She is doing the research that never occurred to me to do myself before agreeing to appear on a *nationally televised show*.

On his show, Dr. Phil pontificates on a spate of topics with which he has little expertise and, in some cases, upon which he is legally prohibited from offering advice. Of course, anyone accepting weight-loss or financial planning tips from a disbarred psychologist . . . gets what they pay for.

I shower, then try on the outfit I've carefully chosen for my date with Phil. Black dress pants, dark purple blouse. First assessment is that I look fatter in L.A. than I did in Minnesota. This is bad. Once the camera gets done adding its requisite ten pounds, Phil will be giving me bunk weight-loss advice and telling me to "get a grip." I take three steps back from the hall mirror and notice a change for the better. Another four steps into the bathroom: even better. Pretty soon, I'm standing on the toilet, as far from my reflection as physically possible, and I'm looking swell indeed.

Mr. DeMille, I'm ready for my close-up. As long as it's not . . . close.

About 10:45 L.A. time, I hit the sack. Room service fish swims in my belly. I could really get used to these two-thousand-thread-count sheets, but I miss my bed, my family, and—for some reason—my therapist.

~

Twelve hours after landing in L.A., I have had a fitful night's sleep and a room service waffle, and now I'm sharing a dressing room with a *guy* named Charlie. This seems odd, but who am I, Angelina Jolie? It's not like I can complain about accommodations. Charlie Cullen is the president of NENA (National Emergency Number Association). We're told we've been placed together due to a shortage of rooms, and because we're on the same side of the issue that's going to be "discussed" on today's show.

The show, we learn, is about 911 dispatch reform, and whether it's needed. The question has been raised by Phil in light of recent 911 calls that have gone poorly, in which people called for help, didn't get it soon enough, and died. Family members of these poor people will be on the show, looking for answers. They will be sitting across from us, looking for answers.

I wasn't the operator for any of these calls, obviously, and neither was Charlie. Yet Charlie and I have been brought to the *Dr. Phil Show* to provide "perspective," to give much-valued "insight," and to shed light on a profession generally shrouded with mystery and misunderstanding.

I think I'm going to hurl.

But first: hair and makeup. The stylist who tackles my hair is small and possibly Puerto Rican. She has done Brooke Shields's hair and knows firsthand that Brooke Shields's mom was a lush. When she finally sets her flat iron down, I do not look like Brooke Shields, but I look darn good, which is a relief.

I am whisked back to my dressing room, where Charlie is taking necktie advice from the wardrobe lady. Someone has left two boxed sandwiches and some strawberries on a table for us. I nibble one berry.

Then, makeup. The makeup guy spends an enormous amount of time on the purple bags under my eyes, but manages to tame them. We don't really converse. I am about thirty minutes away from my brush with Phil. I am about to be on a talk show, watched daily by about four million people. I have forgotten how to make words.

I don't know why I'm here. To support my book, I guess. To be some sort of "expert." But suddenly, this all seems wrong, contrived, and stupid. Four million kinds of stupid.

After a quick hair and makeup check, Charlie and I are brought to a waiting area with several dozen empty chairs and about half a dozen life-sized posters of Phil and the Phamily, which includes Robin McGraw, their two adult sons, and a young blonde who must be a daughter-in-law. Dr. Phil is giving the thumbs-up sign in one, looking contemplative yet confident in another, hands in pockets.

And one other thing: it is about fifty degrees in here.

I thought TV studios were supposed to be hot, with all the lights and cameras and whatnot. Not so at Dr. Phil. I am in Paramount

Studios in downtown L.A., I am one strawberry away from rocket-vomiting, and my nipples are about to fall off from the chill.

About thirty seconds before the show, I meet *The Man.*

Dr. Phil says: "Nice to meet you." Shake, shake. And that's it.

A guy with a gray ponytail and a headset directs me to sit on a couch just left of Phil. Across from me sits the son and the sister of a woman who died due to a potentially botched call for help. The woman is staring angrily at the floor between us. The son's eyes are already misty. His mother's name was Olidia, and she was killed by an armed stalker who brought a gun to her house. She was killed protecting her children from him.

We will listen to a recording of the woman's sister's last moments, in which Olidia called 911 from a cell phone while she was driving and trying to flee her attacker. It is wrenching. The dispatchers are slow to understand what is going on, slow to help her because they are asking some of the wrong questions. But I have been in their shoes and I know they are trying, frustrated, eager to help. But they don't help fast enough, and when Olidia finally reaches a police department, there is nobody ready to help her. Video from the police department shows Olidia running from the man who murdered her, then turned the gun on himself. We will see officers running toward the scene to help, moments too late.

We will all want answers, and none of us will have them.

I won't be able to say on national television: *Sometimes you just don't ask the right questions and sometimes you can't get the whole picture. You could if you had just another minute. But sometimes you don't get another minute.*

God, I'm sorry. I am so sorry.

Suddenly, theme music blasts from enormous speakers. Graphics of phone cords and monitors splash across three large TV screens. Cameras move all around and Ponytail says: Three . . . two . . .

Thankfully, Dr. Phil isn't really looking for answers. He's looking to get his audience whipped up, outraged. It's what he does.

The name of the show? *911 Nightmares.*

~

When the show ended that day, all the guests who were so carefully separated beforehand were hurriedly filed out the same set of doors, TV chattel. Charlie conversed with a man whose wife had died and who was lobbying for increased training for 911 dispatchers. I touched Olidia's sister's elbow, and she turned to me.

I told her I was sorry for what had happened and that I hoped the publicity would inspire some changes for the better. She thanked me. This was the conversation Dr. Phil's staff didn't let us have before the show, or during.

This was the reason Charlie and I had to share a dressing room.

For weeks afterward, my head swims with words I wish I could have said on that stupid show. Like, hey Phil: How about we play just one of the millions of 911 calls that go so brilliantly right every single day?

Why don't we play the one where my partner helped deliver a breech baby two full minutes before the paramedics arrived? Why don't we play the one where my trainer talked an armed suicidal man into putting his gun down and walking peacefully out to the ambulance? Why don't we, Phil?

~

On December 12, 2008, *911 Nightmares* aired, and the Dr. Phil-iverse got a firsthand glimpse at my resting bitch face, my enlarged pores, and my dad's Polish nose.

Oh.

Agony.

In truth, I'm not in the episode much—maybe twenty seconds of actual *Caroline talking* time. That is a mercy. Once I got over what sheer torture it is to see oneself on television, I was able to focus on the real injustice: *911 Nightmares.*

"You looked pissed," a fellow dispatcher told me later. "Like, *really*." And I was. And so were the dispatchers in the audience, who were only shown once, and briefly. Charlie from NENA would promptly write a letter to Dr. Phil expressing his disgust with how dispatchers were portrayed that day and requesting Dr. Phil consider putting together a show featuring some of the heroes of the profession.

Four million people are still holding their breath for that one.

DISPATCHER 1: "Are you talking to me?"

DISPATCHER 2: "No. I'm talking to myself. YOU do it all the time."

DISPATCHER 1: "No, I talk to actual people, but they ignore me. There's a big difference."

15

Souls on Board

In addition to ground ambulances, TAC has *air* ambulance (medical helicopter) bases all over the state, which means instead of knowing just a few square miles of White Bear Lake, population twenty-something thousand, I must now try to gain a working knowledge of . . . the entire state. (We also fly into Wisconsin and the Dakotas and Iowa sometimes.) That's kind of a lot of intersections.

Oh, and by the way: *there are approximately fifteen gazillion First Streets in the state.* So, when a county dispatcher from GodKnows-What County Sheriff's Department calls and orders a ship for the intersection of First Avenue and Main Street, I might first have to look at a list of twenty or more possible locations before I can narrow it down.

"This is Blah Blah County. We need a helicopter for a bus-involved accident to County Road 15 and East County Line."

"Okay, I'm not finding East County Line in my database. Is it called anything else?"

"It's the old Farm Bay Road."

"Is it still called that?"

"I'm not sure. But it's just about four miles north of the Walmart on 15."

"Do you have a proper address for that Walmart?"

"You don't know where Walmart is? How about the Pamida?"

Oh, come on!

Air-ambulance dispatching scares me to death, but not because of the gigantic coverage area.

When you dispatch squads, fire trucks, and ambulances, you try not to send them emergent when it's not necessary, to keep crashes to a minimum. You try to keep track of where they are. Still, crashes happen. Most often, there are only minor injuries. Rarely, there are fatalities.

There is no such thing as a *minor helicopter crash*. If there is a helicopter down, there are no minor injuries. Each ship carries a pilot, a nurse, and a paramedic, and often a patient. Four souls on board, they say.

"Why do they say that? *Souls on board?*" I ask my air-ambulance trainer, Mona, during my first shift in that position. "It's so ominous."

"I don't know," she replies. "But it's better than saying, 'four bodies.' Right?"

Mona is the most senior dispatcher in the center, at thirty-five years and running. So she has been dispatching since somewhere around the year I was born. She can choose any shift she wants, and she always chooses night shift. She comes to each shift with several large bags. Some contain food, some contain newspapers or books to read. She lays out many of these possessions across her console at the start of each shift. So every night, her console has the look of a place that has been hers for years, with papers and pens and chips and plates of watermelon. Even though she must take it all with her when she leaves in twelve hours.

She wears two pairs of glasses most of the time, one in use, the other atop her head. Sometimes both sit atop her head, neither in use. It's cute as hell, and I decide early on to never ask her why, for fear that the answer might be something mundane, or that her reaction will be to stop doing it. To me, she is the sweet, knowledgeable bag-lady/librarian of dispatch sitting at her unkempt workstation and waiting for me to pick her brain, ask for a resource, and just generally *need her*. And holy hell, do I ever need her.

There appears to be nothing about dispatching medical helicopters that rattles her, and I am in awe. Beyond that, she is continually aware of their positioning, able to constantly anticipate what they may need, and *not even the tiniest bit* intimidated by the cocky, rambunctious pilots.

"Air 1 to dispatch."

"Air 1?"

There is a pause. The pilots are used to hearing Mona at this time of night, or Wade or—just about anyone but me.

"Uh, dispatch, I'm going to need LZ [landing zone] info and a ground contact."

"He needs what?"

"For our bus accident. I'll grab him," Mona says patiently.

"Air 1, that will be Chief 312 on MNSef." (This is a special radio channel used when responders from multiple agencies need to communicate.)

"Thanks, Mona."

The pilot's anxiety drops noticeably at the sound of her voice.

"You're welcome."

There is a lot less formality in medical dispatching than in law enforcement, which is taking some time to get used to. And on the night shift, doubly so. (Rumor has it that one night, Mona asked a pilot for a "position" report, and his tongue-in-cheek reply was: "Missionary.")

Maybe it's that fewer medics have military backgrounds than in law enforcement. Maybe it's that cops are so much more serious than just about *anyone*. Still, I look forward to the day when someone is happy to hear my voice on the radio. And, as weirdly informal as it sounds, calls me by name.

Once we have a ship flying, we need to know where it is at all times. Thanks to the miracle of GPS, we can usually see exactly where it is just by looking at a tiny little helicopter moving, slow and steady, across a map. Thanks to human error, GPS doesn't always work. If GPS goes down, then the dispatcher must get a "position report" from the pilot as a latitude and a longitude reading. That way, if a pilot stops answering our calls on the radio and a ship goes missing, we at least have some idea of where that ship may be.

By dispatch edict, we are to obtain these position reports from the pilot at least once every fifteen minutes. Given what's at stake (three or four souls flying through the air at hundreds of miles an hour), positions reports are *kind of a big deal.*

I am reminded of a quote from a New York air traffic controller, featured in the movie *Pushing Tin:* "You land a million planes safely; then you have one little mid-air, and you never hear the end of it."

"We've never had a ship go down," I was told proudly my first week on the job. And that is something to be proud of because not all of our direct competitors can say it. (*You have one little mid-air collision . . .*) It's also something that can trick you, make you think that the worst can't or won't ever actually happen.

~

"700 to Air 1."

"700 . . . Air 1."

"700 calling Air 1."

"700 to Air 3, how do you copy this radio?"

"700, you're loud and clear."

"Copy. 700 to Air 1?"

"Air 3 to 700, where were they going?"

"Air 3, they were en route from north of Kandiyohi to the metro."

"Copy. GPS working?"

"Yes, but they're not moving."

Which is worse than GPS not working.

So, we have five ships, but only know where four of them are. If this were college, we'd be pulling 80 percent, which is still a B-minus.

This is not college, but if we're on a grading system, it is most definitely pass-fail.

By this point, everyone in the room is involved. Everyone is an air-ambulance dispatcher regardless of what position he or she is actually sitting at, and everyone is, just a little bit, pooping his or her ambulance pants. Because we all think it's probably a drill. But maybe it's not. What if it's not?

"Has anyone paged Luke?"

"Who's the air sup tonight?"

"What county is Air 1 in right now?"

"When was their last position?"

Minutes tick by.

Occasionally, our ships fly through areas that are simply radio dead zones, and after ten minutes of our frantic calling, they pop right back on the air like nothing happened. The same can happen with the GPS. This isn't one of those times. I stare intently at the little helicopter on the screen, willing it to begin its tiny crawl once more.

Then we lose another one. Two ships? Sixty percent? That's a D-minus.

Alicia, who was technically the wheelchair dispatcher that day, was the one to notice it.

"We lost Air 2 now, too! It's not moving."

"That's it," Joe announces. "I'm sending squads to look for Air 1."

Those are the magic words. Luke, who has been in his office but within earshot, bounces back into dispatch.

"Don't call them! It's a drill."

I wanna punch somebody.

"I knew it," Alicia says. She has a right to gloat. While the rest of us were fixated on one little spot on the map, Alicia was still looking at the bigger picture. That was apparently a big part of the drill—to see if we would catch that we'd also lost a second ship. Thanks to Alicia, we passed with flying colors.

"I think I'm going to hurl," I announce. Gastrointestinal distress. That's all I have to offer on this particular drill.

We all kind of sit there like zombies for a while afterward. There's a little bit of armchair quarterbacking, a little bit of "Weren't we supposed to page so and so?" and "Don't we do this and not that?" flying around the room. There are five dispatchers who are varying levels of relieved, depending on how many drills each has been through. And there is the knowledge that as much as we hate them, the drills make us better.

One soul. Three souls. Four souls. I never want to forget how much they need me.

～

Mona is the one who doesn't like coffee. The most veteran dispatcher, the veteran *night-shifter. Doesn't like the smell of coffee.*

June (who I believe is just behind Ruth and Mona on the seniority totem pole) clues me in on *the list* the first time Andrew, a newbie they hired shortly after me, tried to bring a bag of microwave popcorn into the dispatch center.

"Oh, you can't have that in here," June gasped, as if he'd brought a basket of rabid hyenas.

"What?"

"I can't stand the smell! Makes me sick."

Confused but compliant, Andrew left with the popcorn.

"We can't have popcorn in here?" I ask, panicked. Popcorn is a full nutrient group on my personal food triangle, nestled right between Frosted Mini-Wheats and Culver's chicken strips.

"You can, but not when I'm here," June said, relaxing again. "Oh, and you can't vacuum when Carl's in here, and when Margaret's here, you can't wear any kind of cologne—You know what? I'll just print you a list."

"Uh. No . . . I'm good."

"I'll print you a list. It'll keep you out of trouble."

"I just want you to know it isn't weird, at all. That you have a list."

"Good! Once you've been here a while you can add something to the list too, if you want," June snickered.

"Can I add something now?"

"Go for it!"

"I can't stand the smell of dusty old day-shift-hogging dispatchers!"

"Oh, Sassypants! You're going to fit *right in*."

"TAC Air, how may I help you?"

"Yes, I live in Minneapolis, and I want to complain about your helicopter flying around this morning."

"Do you mean flying to the hospital? Okay, well, the hospital gets a lot of patients that way."

"Yes, I'm well aware, but your helicopter was flying around and making all kinds of noise at six o'clock in the morning."

"Um, I imagine the pilot was waiting for the pad to clear. So they could land with their *critical patient*."

"Well, next time remind them that there are people who live around here who have rights, too."

"Okay. Would you like to talk about it with our supervisor?"

"No, just tell them what I said."

"Okay. I'll tell the pilot to be quieter next time."

16

Silence

It doesn't pay to get worked up at mean callers in this job.

At some point during my law enforcement days, I took a verbal judo class and learned the fine art of apathy, or, as the instructor called it, "detachment." Whatever you want to call it, it's a simple principle: When an angry caller invites you to get mad, don't bite. Instead, agree with the guy. *They never see that shit coming.*

"What is taking them so fucking long?" a caller with back spasms asks me.

"They had to divert to a heart-related call," I explain.

"Whatever. Tell them I want to go to Regions."

"They will take you wherever you would like. Just let them know."

"Last week, they said they would only take me to County."

"They will take you wherever you would like." *Is this thing on?*

"Last time they took forever to get here, too."

"I'm sure that was really frustrating."

"Next time, I'm going to call someone else."

"Well, you certainly have that right, sir."

See? I truly don't give a shit. I'm so detached, I'm barely breathing. It's super freeing.

The best way to handle a hysterical caller, I'm learning, is to not say anything at all. I was trained early on that if your caller won't stop yelling or screaming, you repeat the same thing in the same tone of voice three times. It's a decent first step.

"Mary, please calm down so we can help you."

"Mary, please calm down so we can help you."

"Mary blah, blah blah, blah help you."

But if this doesn't work, there's only one thing left to do: shut the hell up.

They never see that shit coming.

"Hello? Hello?"

"Yes, I'm here."

"Is someone coming?"

Sometimes callers believe that because they are still talking to someone, nobody is en route to help yet. As in, *how can you be coming to help me if we're still talking?*

"They've been on the way since you first called. Will you let me ask some questions now?"

"What kind of questions?"

"Like, is he breathing?" *You know, silly shit.*

The public at large probably doesn't want to hear the words *apathy* and *detachment* associated with emergency services. It's okay. Imagine Halle Berry clutching a stress ball and hyperventilating into her headset over every call, if that makes you feel better. But if I am ever a customer again, I'll take the Zen dispatcher, if you please.

So, to the extent that I am able, I verbal-judo the shit out of my callers.

What's that, ma'am? I'm the worst call-taker you've ever heard of? *I couldn't agree more. Stand by for a moment of silence.*

"Sir, is your friend completely alert?"

"No, but I mean, he's not the brightest guy normally, anyway."

17

Baby in a Pond

Somewhere around my third year as a dispatcher, I discovered yoga. A yoga classroom is the antithesis of a dispatch center. There is no chatter in yoga. There is no chirping, no beeping, no squelching, and no screaming.

There is no time-stamping. There is no crosstalk and no backtalk. There are no transmissions, no calls on hold, and with the exception of the occasional chime, there is no ringing. *Nothing* is emergent in yoga.

I started practicing beginner yoga on DVD when I was in my early thirties, after a doctor showed me an X-ray of the arthritis in my lower back. It seemed very unfair to be getting arthritis before ever getting my first gray hair, but now that I have both, plus the occasional pimple, I realize that age is a laughing hyena that just keeps cackling louder and louder until we go deaf and then die.

Anyway, yoga helps loosen up the arthritis in my lower back. Yoga is non-critical. I can pay $15 to lie on my back for the whole damn hour if that's what I want to do. I am allowed to royally suck at yoga. If I can't twist one way or bend another way, nobody is going to die. Maybe I'll get injured. If I get injured, I can still dispatch.

Sometimes, on a slow night shift (which is all of them, eventually), I'll take off my headset and go into a downward-facing dog pose. (It's basically an upside-down V with both hands and both feet on the floor.) It gets the blood flowing to the head and wakes me up.

It gives my wrists something to do that doesn't involve slowly developing carpal tunnel syndrome. If I'm feeling really ambitious (or really bored), I'll go into a headstand. I have to be very careful about where I do this. A poorly placed headstand dismount could land my feet into a cluster of monitors and wires. The thought of explaining this kind of gymnastics to the boss saps the happy chi right out of me.

In yoga, I don't have to be focused on anything but my breathing. In dispatching, I'm supposed to be focused on everything, all the time.

"Tell me exactly what happened."

"Someone just found my grandson in the pond."

"He fell in?"

"Well, I guess so."

"Is he awake?"

"I don't . . . uh. Hold on. *I'm on the phone with them right now!*"

"Sir? Sir, I need you to talk to me. Is he breathing?"

When talking to a caller who is in the midst of a large gathering of people, I sometimes have to get all *sir* or *ma'am* on his or her ass. I'm just a little voice on the phone, and it's important that I have my caller's undivided attention. Calling him a name he almost never goes by in a voice that probably reminds him of his least-favorite elementary-school teacher is a half-baked plan, really, and rarely works. But it's all I've got. If blow horns weren't so disruptive, most of us would really benefit from the surprise factor. In their absence, we have *schoolteacher voice.*

"Sir!"

What follows are several long minutes of my unsuccessful attempts to get Sir's attention, interspersed with the panicked input of several partygoers asking my caller where the hell the ambulance is.

This is my third toddler-involved drowning, and it appears to be very much in the way the first two did. I am unable to hold my caller's attention so that we can start CPR. Maybe both of those children were beyond help when the calls came in. Maybe this one is beyond help too, but *sweet baby Jesus* I would give my right ear to get someone pumping his chest. As it is, I can't even get the guy to tell me if his grandson is breathing.

The police arrive, and I am disconnected. I'm pretty sure that the last five minutes have undone about two year's worth of yoga benefits. I am *wound up*.

To start with, my breathing is all wrong, and I'm warm. And the harder I try to return my breath and my temperature to normal, the worse I get. This is not my first panic attack. But the thing about panic attacks is that they cause you to *panic*, which doesn't lend itself to good reasoning skills, and it doesn't help you remember that you lived through the last one.

I'm a perfectly healthy woman in her mid-thirties with a queasy stomach and some lightheadedness. I'm also running on about four hours of sleep. So of course I think I'm having some sort of *major cardiac event*. I want to step out, but I see that Danielle already has. While I had been stressing out over what I couldn't get the grandfather to do, Danielle had been having her very own hard time with the same scene, talking to the mother. Neither of us knew we had the same call going at the same time until afterward.

Danielle is seven months pregnant, plus the mother of a toddler. Of course that would have been a hard call for her. But what's *my* problem?

Thanks to the seating configuration, my partner, Margaret, is the only dispatcher who can actually see me. But she does see me. Oh, and she's a paramedic.

She takes in my pale skin and look of agony.

"What's wrong with you?"

"I don't feel so great."

"Are you having chest pain?"

"I don't know . . ." *Cardiac event, people.*

"I'm paging a crew."

Damn it. As is oft the case, there is a two-paramedic ambulance crew already in the building. That's the good and bad thing about working with helpers. They're such *helpy helpers.* I can't argue with Margaret. It wouldn't do any good, anyway.

The security door swings open, and it's a medic named Lizzie, who looks about eighteen years old to me, plus a male paramedic I've never met, and *(sure, why not?!)* a stretcher.

They whisk me onto the stretcher and wheel me past my alarmed dispatch cohorts and down the hallway toward the parking lot, where the ambulance is parked with its rear doors already open. The street supervisor, Mort, is holding the last door to the outside with a grim look of concern. Lizzie is asking me questions while placing small, sticky pads (called 12-leads) to various parts of my upper body, and I'm pretty sure that if I die on this particular shift, it will not be from a cardiac event, *it will be from embarrassment.*

"Okay, what hospital do you want to go to?" Lizzie says, securing the stretcher to the floor of the ambulance.

"None!" I say, with much gusto. I do not want to go to any hospital. Stop the EMS train; *I wanna get off.*

Plus, I'm feeling better. Because the great thing about panic attacks is that they always end. And one stellar way to end *my* panic attacks is to give me something else to focus on, like how badly I don't want to go to the ER.

Lizzie is perturbed. She has wasted what feels like no fewer than twenty of those 12-leads on my non-cardiac-event-having ass. "You don't think you should get checked?"

"No, I'm good. I don't think it's serious. I just felt so awful for a minute there."

"Are you okay now?" Lizzie asks. It's not a cardiac question, but a question from a warrior who has seen much worse than I have, and still cares.

I'm never actually surprised when I feel bad after something terrible has happened to a child, or anyone for that matter. When I think about it, I should be surprised when I *don't* feel bad.

"I'm okay," I say.

My breathing is back to normal, and my color has gone from terrified white to a friendlier tone of light fuchsia.

I skulk back into the building. First, I head to the bathroom to discreetly remove all the sticky pads from my boobs and various other parts. That Lizzie's a 12-lead *ninja*. I wash my face. I'm a new dispatcher.

"You're back!" Margaret exclaims when I slide sheepishly into my seat.

"This is where all the fun is!"

"Oh. Is it really?"

"They transported your drowning."

"Code 3?"

"Routine."

"What?"

The child didn't die. In fact, the child was never not breathing. I didn't actually hear what I heard, and neither did Danielle. It felt great to be so utterly, embarrassingly . . . wrong.

For the rest of the shift, I focus on my breathing. Partially because it feels good, and partially because two panic attacks in one shift is probably frowned upon.

Yoga means union. I focus on the union between myself and the people I work with. I find one last 12-lead still stuck to me under my bra and know that even though I'm not perfect, I'm safe and cared for, and about three minutes from getting chucked into the back of an ambulance *at any point.*

These are some of the best people I'll ever know.

"Hey, Caroline, you want in on a crave case?"

"No. Not now, not ever."

"Come on. Want some fries? You liked the fries last time, right?"

"Yes, I did. But I'm scared."

"Aw. Why you scared?"

"Because when you guys get White Castle, you fart your onion-burger farts all night."

"And it makes you crave White Castle?"

"I'll take a small fry, and this time I'm propping the door open."

"As you wish."

18

The Dispatch Diet

Meg is another of the former switchboard ladies. A member of the thirty-plus club. She is a kind and compassionate call-taker and a precise and deliberate dispatcher. She is known for using spray margarine on her toast in the mornings. It's kind of cute, but I can't fathom how that can be good.

Anyway, hers is the best banana-cake recipe I've ever known.

Meg's banana cake is moist like a Twinkie. I'm pretty sure it's the four ripe bananas and all that shortening. It's a mix-and-bake type of recipe. You can't mess it up. *I* can't mess it up. That's saying something. You can find the recipe in the dispatch recipe files, which we all have access to, along with dozens of others. Rhubarb bread. Chicken pot pie. Watergate cake. You know, healthy fare.

I don't even need the written banana cake recipe anymore, I've made it so many times. Here it is, from memory:

2 cups of flour
1½ teaspoons of baking powder
1½ teaspoons of baking soda
1 teaspoon of salt
1⅔ cups of sugar
3 eggs
⅔ cup of shortening
4 ripe bananas, crushed

    1 cup of buttermilk
    1 bag o' chocolate chips

(Meg's official recipe doesn't call for chocolate chips, but every version I've seen has them. In my opinion, they're critical. Chocolate generally is.)

Mix the dry ingredients first, then add all but the chips and blend on medium speed for three minutes. Fold in chips. Bake in a greased 9 × 13 pan at 350 degrees for 50 minutes. If you forget to grease the pan, don't worry. You can just eat the whole warm, gooey mess right out of the pan and not serve it to anyone else. Experience talking here.

But if you want to make some friends, bring it to dispatch, cut it into smallish pieces, put down a stack of napkins, and back away slowly. We love to eat.

There is a term for what happens as a result of all the eating: dispatcher spread. Dispatcher spread is the slow and steady widening of our thighs and waistlines, and the accompanying shrinking of our chairs. We all must learn the hard way that ambulance pants don't stretch. Off the top of my head, I can think of four dispatchers who have had some sort of weight-loss surgery that either sucked something out, cinched something up, or was otherwise intended to lead to losing weight.

Culver's Restaurant is a quarter mile away, and most of us can find the frozen custard "flavor of the day" faster than we can remember our own work schedules.

Sometimes, it's the boredom that causes the constant grazing. Popcorn, if eaten in moderation, is pretty light. If grazed upon between calls over a twelve-hour shift, it is a Culver's bacon cheeseburger to the gut.

Sometimes, a well-timed Snickers bar can keep you just conscious enough to be ready for bar rush. Twenty-seven grams of sugar is generally good for thirty-forty minutes of buzz.

"Guess what?" It is 6:00 P.M., Richard has just sat down next to me, and we are both in the first hours of our respective twelve-hour night shifts. I can never *guess what* correctly. I'm in the *must know* business.

"What?"

"You're supposed to guess."

"I hate this game."

Richard pouts, which looks weird on a guy his age. Richard is not the oldest dispatcher in our center, but because he works the night shift with a bunch of disrespectful miscreants, he has collected such nicknames as "Old Man River" and "Grampa."

"Okay. Is it animal, vegetable, or mineral?"

"It's bakery."

"I love this game."

"My wife made butterhorns."

I own three different sizes of polyester pants. Size eight, size ten, and size butterhorn.

"Your wife makes me wish I had a wife."

"I'm a pretty lucky guy."

"Where are they?"

"Not just yet! Have some patience. Go stand on your head or whatever it is you do."

Butterhorns are soft, lovely rolls made—of course—with a lot of butter. Richard's wife also pours a sweet glaze over each roll, a glaze made with powdered sugar and probably cocaine, because after I've had one I generally want to dance a jig on the console. Then, when I realize they are all gone, I want to crawl all over dispatch looking for butterhorn crumbs in the carpet.

Unfortunately, butterhorns also make the phone ring. It never fails. The moment I'm handed one, the *damn phone rings*.

"This is Blah Blah County with a transfer on someone thrown from a horse. We're staging at County Road 9 and Old Bay Road. Can you get a helicopter started?"

"Okay, Air 1 to 9 and Old Bay," I say, knowing that Richard has also set his butterhorn down and is waiting to see what I've got on the line. He *set his butterhorn down*. Old man has discipline.

"Sir, can you tell me what happened?"

"I don't know . . . I was behind her too far. But she's on the ground."

"Is she awake?"

"Yeah, she's yelling."

"That's good! Keep her very still."

Thanks to Richard, the helicopter almost beats the ambulance to the remote riding path where my caller and his wife wait for help. I never learn the outcome, but a screaming patient is a live patient.

Saving lives and eating sweets. It's what we do, and we do it well.

I've never asked Richard's wife for the butterhorn recipe. They have kind of an inaccessible taste, like something I couldn't replicate on my own. A little too complex and mysterious.

Watergate cake, on the other hand, I can handle. That's one of Mona's, and the two main ingredients are already junk foods in their own right: box cake mix and instant pistachio pudding. Delightfully easy. It's like eating a green Twinkie with nuts.

Note: None of these dispatchers claim to have invented these recipes, nor will they take responsibility if these recipes cause your own version of dispatcher spread.

Follow the dispatch diet at your own risk.

"Sir, can you tell me exactly what happened?"

"Listen, I've got this heart thing. Well, wait. It goes back to when I was . . ."

"Can you tell me what happened tonight, that made you call?"

"Well, Angel, I wanted to speak with someone just like you."

"Okay. What's wrong?"

"I got . . . well, first of all, I should tell you that I've had a cocktail or two."

"Okay."

"But it's not that. It's that my heart hurts, Angel. And not just because I'm talking to *you*."

19

Open Mic Night

Nearly everything we do is recorded. Every phone call, whether it comes in on an emergent or non-emergent line, is recorded and sent to some cloud of memory somewhere so it can be recalled, reviewed, or rehashed somewhere down the line. Sometimes for legal reasons, sometimes for evaluation, sometimes for shits and giggles. Every utterance on the radio gets the same treatment.

Sometimes those recordings end up as fodder for department training. One of my proudest moments was when a life-save I helped with got the spotlight as an example of "what to do." Conversely, if your performance is less than stellar, it can end up as a "learning tool." That's more of a head-to-the-desk type of moment. Which has also happened to me.

If one of us has a really memorable moment on the phone or radio, it can end up on the department "blooper reel."

"Okay, ma'am, before we get there, don't forget to put away any pets, dogs, cats, or . . . chickens you may have."

"Air 2, I copied you're arrived and in the ground. *On* the ground. I mean you're *on* the ground."

Sometimes, things are said into a live microphone by accident. There are three different ways to transmit. One is by mouse-clicking specific talkgroups on the monitor. Another is by stepping on a pedal on the floor. Another button rests on a pack-set on the dispatcher's waistband. This particular button is just *begging* to be unknowingly leaned into, nudged, or otherwise tripped, allowing any number of ill-advised comments to be broadcast on the radio. Sometimes the microphone just gets stuck open and won't close until we reboot the computer.

When an open mic happens, it's usually noticed first by another dispatcher in the room, who yells, "Open mic!" in the hopes of stopping the insanity.

"Did 103 copy me? He's being such an asshole today."

"Open mic!"

Or . . .

"I have a gassy chassis today."

"And you just told everyone on the metro talkgroup."

Sometimes we use the fear of the open mic against each other.

"Is that Johnson on 502? He's such a loser."

"Open mic!"

"Shit!"

"Just kidding."

One Sunday morning, I happened to be part of an all-female team of dispatchers, which is somewhat rare. (Usually it's about half and half.) I only tell you that part so you don't judge us too harshly when I tell you that we were looking at *Pure Romance* catalogs and talking about dildos for the better part of an hour.

We were absolutely, undeniably doing our jobs. But in between doing our jobs, when the phones weren't ringing, we were absolutely talking about dildos.

"Which one are you looking at?" said one dispatcher to another.

"The rainbow rabbit" came the reply.

"What the hell is a . . ."

"Look! This one."

At about *rainbow rabbit* is when I started hearing the conversation in both my free ear and the one with the ear bud.

"What about the 'like a virgin'?"

And then, louder than all the other transmissions: "It's supposed to make you tighter."

"Open mic!" I yelled finally.

Nobody saved that for the blooper reel.

Ahem.

Dispatcher to dispatcher, during shift change:
"So, what ya got for me, ya little effer?"
"Um. An open mic."
"Shit."
"Yeah . . . still open."

20

Mothers

Mothers who call about their children can be *challenging*. Mothers tend to care way too much, yell way too much, freeze up, or try so hard to control the outcome that they get in the way or make things worse. I'm not judging; I'm a mother cut from that same cloth.

I'm thinking of a mom who called one day, her choking toddler in her arms, panting and interrupting me as I tried to assess what was going on so I could help.

"Ma'am, what is she choking on?" I ask, knowing she probably didn't hear it. Is she running with the baby? That's what it sounds like. I also hear a baby crying, which would be a great sign, breathing-wise, but experience has taught me I can't assume it's the right baby.

I ask again, "What is she choking on?"

"I slapped her on the back!" she announces, and now I'm *really* worried.

Never, never, NEVER slap a choking person on the back. There's a scene in *Field of Dreams* that makes me cringe every time I see it. A little girl watching a baseball game falls off the stands and begins to choke on a hot dog, but thankfully, there is a "doctor" right there (played by the irrepressible Burt Lancaster)! He pauses as though he's lining up his next great golf swing, pulls his hand back, and *thud, thud*, right in the middle of her back. Out comes the hot dog.

"She'll be turning handsprings before you know it," he tells Cost-ner's character, tossing the offending hot dog piece nonchalantly.

No. No, no, no. A thousand times *no*.

"Do NOT slap her on the back anymore," I tell her. Then I say it again, because she's still talking over me.

"What do I *do*?" she says, and I take that as my cue to ask her some questions and perhaps get her going with some compressions. But before I can do that, an officer arrives. You're probably wondering what happened. I can tell you with 99 percent certainty that the baby was fine because I don't really remember any further details. The handful of *baby not fine* calls I have taken stay with me.

Ingestions are a big deal with mothers; it's upsetting to imagine that your child has eaten something inedible, and nobody wants to be that mother who just stood by while her child died of (fill in the blank) poisoning.

"My son drank some Windex!"

"My daughter ate a funny-looking berry!"

These calls rarely come from dads. This is not a statement that dads are careless or that moms are overly cautious, but it's a true statement nonetheless. If a dad is making this kind of call, it's usually because the mom is too upset about *fill in the blank* poisoning to make the call herself.

I picture my dad's reaction to my older brother or me upon having eaten any inedible thing: "Oh, it's nothing to worry about. Puts hair on your chest!" (Which, in his estimation, is a good thing.)

As a mother myself, no matter how benign the object or fluid, I always err on the side of caution with these calls. Per protocol, I get an ambulance rolling, then put mom through to the fine folks at Poison Control. Ingestion *is their business*.

Dispatcher: "Poison Control? I have a mom on the line whose eighteen-month-old son ate a pencil eraser. I'll stay on the line."

"Dispatch, do you have an ambulance going on this?"

"Yes, one is started."

"Cancel it."

"Copy, canceling."

I know what you're thinking, but I don't want to be the one dispatcher who didn't start an ambulance and then the little guy dies of PEP. (Pencil eraser poisoning; I just made that up.) No, thanks. "You've never heard of PEP? Didn't you hear about that one case in Florida?" Okay, so PEP isn't actually a thing. I Googled it. But we don't have time to Google stuff in dispatch. And I'm pretty sure confidence in us would decline rapidly if we started dispatching by *Google search*. "Sir, go ahead and stick some bubble gum in that gunshot wound. No, it's cool. I Googled it. Puts hair on your chest."

~

When I mine my mental database for mothers who were notably *not* hysterical, I can only really remember one mother, and maybe it's because her baby was not fine at all. She had been giving her baby a bath, she told me, and stepped away. When she returned, her baby was under the water.

She stepped away? For how long? And *why*? And those are the things part of me wanted to ask, but the larger part of me wanted to get that baby breathing again because, as the mother had told me calmly, she wasn't.

Sometimes adrenaline kicks in and gives you exactly what you need, and sometimes adrenaline gives you so much of what you need, you trip on it. In my haste to get to the right instructions for baby CPR, I had entered something wrong, and my instructions wouldn't come up. But I knew enough to get her going on compressions, so I just went from memory.

"Ma'am, I need you to get the baby on a hard surface."

But she wouldn't get going.

"Ma'am, can you hear me okay?"

Instead, she told me again what had happened and asked me what to do.

But I was trying to tell her.

"Ma'am? Let's get going on compressions."

She was *so* calm. I didn't make a lot of assumptions about it; a mother in shock, *or anyone* in shock, can be really hard to reach. What if I were called on to give my own child CPR? Would I perform? Would I freeze? Most of us in this profession like to think we wouldn't. But I really don't know.

The baby died. Drowned, to be specific.

I learned later that an investigation was started on the mother. I followed some of it in the newspapers. I never learned what became of her, though.

What stays with me is the baby.

~

Being a mother and a dispatcher can be a challenging combination as well. I know all the worst possible outcomes of any situation. I've never owned, operated, or even been a passenger on a snowmobile, but I've had only negative experiences with them, by phone. Nobody ever calls me when they have a safe and successful ride on a snowmobile, just when someone's been thrown from one, driven one into a lake, or something equally calamitous. As a result, I don't like snowmobiles. It's a grudge, I guess . . . an *educated prejudice.*

I also don't like:

ATVs

or motorcycles

or teenage drivers

or drunk drivers

or icy roads

or four-way stop signs

or large crowds

or small crowds

or any city in which a sex offender resides (which is all of them)

or rap concerts

or country music festivals

or anything that can impale something (which is almost everything)

or disembodied heads (for obvious reasons).

I could go on.

Imagine that I'm your mom. Actually, imagine that both your parents are dispatchers, which was my daughter's fate for darn near five years, most of those years as a high school student.

"Hey, can I go to Suzy's grandpa's cabin with her this weekend?"

"Where is it?"

"I don't know. Like up by McGregor?"

"I'm going to need an address and what county it's in. And preferably what agency patrols it."

"Huh?"

"I'm also going to need Suzy's grandpa's full name and date of birth. Has he always lived in Minnesota?"

"How would I . . ."

"And what are you going to do at this alleged cabin?"

"Well, her grandpa has snowmobiles and stuff . . ."

"You don't know how to operate a snowmobile. I'm pretty sure nobody does."

"I drove one at Jenny's house!"

"You . . . what? And didn't ask me?"

"You would have said no."

"Damn right. And now you're grounded."

～

One afternoon, three weeks after my daughter got her driver's license, I get a phone call at home.

I had planned to take a nap with Jim, but instead stayed up to tinker until Mariah got back. She had taken her '93 Honda Accord to the Walgreens about one mile from our house twenty minutes earlier, and I was still in *waiting for my kid's safe return* mode when it came to this new phase of her independence. She had looked so cute with her plaid summer purse and her *I'm driving myself* giddiness.

The number on the caller ID was not one I recognized. When I picked up, he just said, "Are you Mariah's mom?"

"Yes . . ."

"She's been in an accident. There's a little bit of blood, but she's okay." She was okay enough to give someone our number to call. Yet . . . there's a little bit of blood? I hear my daughter yelling and crying in the background.

As a law-enforcement major, Jim has had training in driving like a crazed maniac for emergency purposes. The accident was only four or five blocks away, and even though he had woken from a dead sleep just minutes earlier, it felt like he beamed us there in his Taurus. And when we arrived, we were dumbfounded.

Her car was halfway under a school bus.

It was an accident I probably could have had a hundred times as a teenage driver. A little too much speed on a usually open road, a moment reaching for a water bottle, and she had rear-ended a vehicle with a bumper too high to repel her little car. So she was under it, and trapped.

She had a two- or three-inch gash just above her hairline. There was *a lot* of blood.

Already, there were several squad cars and firefighters on the scene. A civilian, who we later learned was an off-duty paramedic, had immediately placed himself in the backseat of the demolished car, and despite the broken glass, blood, and chaos, was keeping Mariah's neck stable with just his two bare hands. My daughter was panicked, screaming, and stunned all at once.

If there's an upset-mother spectrum, 1 being apathetic and 10 being hysterical, I was at 11 on the inside.

I watched in a daze as men and women I mostly knew only from the other end of a radio worked to free my daughter from her crushed vehicle. Firefighters scurried here and there, pulling out equipment, talking about ETAs, extrication, landing zones . . .

Landing zone? My stomach lurched. They had ordered a helicopter. Logically, I knew a helicopter was appropriate for this situation. But it completely freaked me out that *a helicopter was appropriate for this situation.*

"They're going to have her out of there soon," said an officer from just behind me. I was trembling and crying. I turned to see Officer O'Neil from good old White Bear Lake PD, and I'd never been so glad to see that old crab-ass in all my life.

"All that yelling is good. But you know that."

As I watched, stunned, the men and women of White Bear Lake Fire Department used the Jaws of Life to crack open Mariah's car like a tuna can. They carefully delivered her onto a stretcher and placed her into an ambulance (the helicopter was canceled). Jim hopped in with her and they drove away, lights flashing, sirens blaring.

I couldn't feel my feet.

If I had been in any kind of shape for it, this would have been a terrific learning experience. Here was just about every form of help I could ever need to dispatch, all on the same scene. It didn't occur to me until much later how quickly everyone had arrived.

And how many people on how many cell phones had called that one-person dispatch center to report the accident? My head hurt to think of it.

Later, in the intensive-care unit, as Jim and I watched our stitched, sedated, bruised, but miraculously whole and healthy daughter sleep, I thought about how she looked that day when she left for the store, her perfect eyeliner, her smiling blue eyes, her trendy plaid purse—so proud just to be driving herself to Walgreens.

She might have died.

I swore I was going to personally thank the dispatcher who was working that day. I wanted to tell her she was not forgotten, and that her hard work saved my daughter. Of course, I never did. I never gave her the awkwardly long hug she so richly deserves.

This is a late, but heartfelt thank-you.

Thanks to her, today my daughter is a living, breathing, special-ed major with a bright future and a bus pass.

Thanks to her, this mom still has a daughter to get hysterical about.

"911?"

"He's gone, he's gone, he's gone!"

"Who's gone? Tell me what happened?"

"He's on the bed and he's gone! My baby! My baby."

"Do you know what happened? Ma'am? Can you hear me?"

"Oh no, oh no!"

"Ma'am, please tell me what happened?"

"Oh no, oh no, oh no."

21

The Call

There isn't much out there about dispatching, movie-wise (or on TV, or in literature). So, it was super exciting to hear that a movie *about a 911 dispatcher* was in the works, and that it was going to feature the always lovely, sometimes sassy, Oscar-winning actress Halle Berry. It was a thriller, aptly titled *The Call*, and I saw it in the theater in its first week. Which is good, because it wasn't in theaters long.

Berry plays Jordan, a lithe and pert-nosed 911 veteran who can dispatch a husband/wife shooting call with the same calm indifference as she would announce a noise complaint. At least that is the case until she picks up the prowler-in-progress call that catapults her into *the rising action and thrilling plot!*

It is during that prowler-in-progress call that Jordan makes a mistake that costs a young girl her life. For the purposes of this chapter, I watched the whole thing over again at home. It still gives me the heebs.

Broken, Jordan retreats into the safe haven of training other dispatchers until one night she is pulled back in, and it is the exact same type of call. And—by Hollywood coincidence—it is even the same prowler. Jordan's caller, a young girl named Casey, has been kidnapped and thrown into the trunk of a car. With her phone. I know, right? *Redemption, party of one?*

Halle Berry is our own personal David Caruso. (Cue *The Who*.)

Which leads us to my favoritest part of *The Call*, the holy-shit, nail-chewing several-minute sequence in which Jordan masterfully keeps Casey calm and helps her find new and awesome ways to help attract attention to the kidnapper's car so police can locate it.

I've saved actual lives and delivered actual babies. And I don't know if I found the reality even half as thrilling as watching Halle Berry save a fictional life for millions of viewers. Because here's the thing: Whether this kind of shit ever actually happens, there was Halle Berry up on the silver screen making everyone think that it does. Making everyone see a dispatcher as a hero.

We so rarely get to be the heroes we so often are. I've never met a single person that I've helped. In the senior prom of emergency services, dispatchers are the mousy, bespectacled debate-team girls glued to the gymnasium wall, hoping somebody will notice that we got our hair done and spent some money on a dress.

I don't know many dispatchers who haven't seen *The Call*. And though most will concede that it was mostly bullshit, most will say they loved it. You know the adage that any pizza is good pizza? Well, any dispatch movie is a good dispatch movie. Because—it's a dispatch movie.

Six months earlier, I took a call on a five-year-old shot in the back. My caller was surrounded by family and chaos and couldn't hear me. It was basically three minutes of screaming.

"Ma'am? Ma'am? Ma'am, can you tell me what's happened?"

"He's been shot!"

"Ma'am where is the shooter? Where is the gun? Ma'am? Ma'am?"

I was of no help. That is very typical. It's not that I don't have helpful things to tell her, helpful things to advise her to do for him. It's that she is unable to hear me. It's not her fault. Someone dear to her has been *shot*.

Someone else sent the cops, someone else drove the ambulance, and someone else met the medics and the patient at the ER. I am the mousy girl, glued to the wall, listening to the most horrible school dance ever, on a cell phone. I guess I should consider myself lucky.

If Halle Berry had answered that call, she would have said something to grab that woman's attention. Once she had her attention, she would have instructed her to place a clean, dry cloth or towel directly on the wound. She would have stopped the bleeding long enough to keep him stable and breathing until help arrived. They would have rushed him to the ER, and it would have been soon enough. All the sirens, all the hand-wringing, all the hope, and all the rushing—it all would have been enough for a happy Hollywood ending, and she would have saved that little guy, who was just busy being a five-year-old in his own house, busy minding his own little life, and was no part of any gang.

This would have been so much better in a Halle Berry movie.

In the movies, someone would have been caught and brought to justice. Maybe we would get to see his dumbstruck face when they declared him "Guilty!" Maybe we would get to hear the satisfying *ga-gong* of the prison bars moving into place, locking him away forever.

Halle Berry would have had a tearful hospital-room meeting with that beautiful boy and his mom, and it would be okay that awful things happen, because when they happen to little children in cinema, it's never the end. They can come back.

In the movies, we are not endlessly powerless.

In the movies, we have more choices than whether to go to the debriefing or not to go to the debriefing, or whether to go to the funeral or not to go to the funeral. Why go? Three minutes of screaming.

Don't be so sensitive. Don't let it get to you.

Okay, if you don't want the movie spoiled for you, then you better stop right here.

Because it ends with Jordan getting out from behind her console and going right the hell out into the big bad world to save Casey. Why didn't she send the cops, you ask?

Why do they get to have all the fun?

She tracks him down to his *Silence of the Lambs*–esque lair, where we get to see a smoking-hot dispatcher in a wife-beater save a young girl's life and kick some bad-guy ass. The only thing missing is her American flag–inspired cape.

Sometimes, if you love the idea behind a movie enough, you can just suspend your disbelief out of sheer, unaltered *joy.*

"You're just an operator," our villain tells Jordan during their insanely implausible final encounter. "You can't do this!"

"It's already done," she replies.

Booyah.

DISPATCHER 1: "Did you fart?"

DISPATCHER 2: "No! I NEVER do that in the comm center."

DISPATCHER 1: "In something like fifteen years, you've never let one go in the comm center."

DISPATCHER 2: "Never. Not once. If I have to toot, I step out."

DISPATCHER 1: "Dude. I've farted five times in, like, half an hour."

22

Active Shooter

On the evening of April 20, 1999, I was in a Kia dealership looking at a Sportage mini-SUV with a five-speed and a rag top. I was thinking what a bad idea it was to buy this car. We really couldn't afford the payment on a brand-new anything, even if it was a Kia. Plus, I'd never owned a rag top, and that just seemed like a bad idea in Minnesota.

When the breaking news about Columbine High School popped up on the dealership TV mounted high up in the lobby, everything stopped for the evening. How many shot? Who did this? Why? We watched with a combined sense of horror and detachment. Images of Dylan Klebold and Eric Harris looked to me like gangly, armed teenagers—walking on the moon. Not here, not ever.

At the time, I was working at a large law publisher and editing law citations on the afternoon shift, and I still thought that the biggest challenge of the new millennium would be getting all of our computers to read the correct time. I had no idea that fourteen years later, school shootings would be so frequent that I would struggle to remember them individually. And the biggest challenge of the new millennium? Getting kids to stop killing each other.

I never would have guessed on that night in 1999 that I would find myself in a classroom twelve years later, watching a video of kids being shot in the halls of their own high school.

The video was not real, of course. It was an active-shooter training session, and the students were actors. A blond, shaggy-haired, white teenage boy had made his way into his high school with a semiautomatic weapon and was shooting everyone he came in contact with. This wasn't a made-for-TV movie, so we, the viewers, were not spared much detail. This wasn't made to help us believe in happy endings.

When a cop is trained on how to use a Taser gun, he or she is generally required to take a shot of Taser juice as well. Same with mace. In some small way, I felt Tased by that video. It was somebody's effort to toughen me to the whole active-shooter thing, to make me feel some of the fear and horror those kids and their teachers would certainly feel in that situation.

Mission accomplished. Still, I didn't feel any more *prepared*.

Nobody in emergency services ever wants to hear the words *active shooter*. The shooter part is bad enough. The active part is redundant, really. But it's there to remind us that what has happened is still happening. An active shooter could be anywhere. An active shooter could be at a warehouse or a college campus or even a marathon. An active shooter is moving and randomly shooting innocent people. There may be more than one shooter, and there may be explosives.

And each second spent trying to figure out where to stage the medics, deciding where to send the officers, agreeing on who to call for mutual aid, scrambling to find an aerial view of the building, trying to get information from callers, panicking, sweating, or just plain trying to think rationally—means actual lives. Often it means the lives of children.

None of us ever wants to be put in that position.

But one morning, we got a call. There was an active shooter in a rural middle school in one of the many areas we cover for ambulance and air care. There were shots fired and students injured, and that's all we were told because that's all anybody knew for at least the first hour.

An officer once told me his theory on why it's okay for emergency-services people to have downtime (you know, donut time—time to shoot the shit and drink coffee). He said sometimes we're being paid not for what we are doing but for what we could be called upon to do at any moment. He was eating a donut at the time. But I agree.

Because the active-shooter call? It was a hoax. It was a twelve-year-old trying to get out of a big math test, perhaps, or dodge ball day in gym class. There were no shots fired and, mercifully, no injuries.

Huge relief, right? But for about ninety minutes, there was no relief. There were just ninety minutes of knowing that hundreds of parents were praying for their children. Ninety minutes believing that kids could be hurt or killed. Ninety minutes in suspended animation. It felt like a betrayal to all of those kids and their families to relax for even a moment of it, to take our eyes off the monitors in front of us, to think about anything else, or to stop trying to anticipate what would be needed next.

All lines, emergent or non-emergent, were answered on the first ring. No bathroom breaks. Radio transmissions were kept brief. Conversations in the comm center were short and low volume. Just waiting and listening.

When it was over and we got the all-clear, it *was* a relief. But not just for the obvious reasons. In essence, it was our first ever *active-shooter drill*, and we'd pretty much kicked ass. We'd used the right frequencies, we'd called the right people, and we'd forgotten nothing. We'd staged all the responders correctly, and we'd waited like good dispatchers.

We'd stood guard and waited when we were needed. It was a ninety-minute training more valuable than any graphic video or classroom lesson we could have ever taken. We felt prepared for a mass school shooting. We felt ready for multiple victims, mass casualties, explosives.

And that felt great, and it felt awful.

"911?"

"Yes, I'd like you to send someone out to get rid of the people under my house. They're back."

"Are you sure?"

"Oh, yes. Yes, I'm very sure. I can hear them talking and laughing and all of that."

"Okay, Mrs. Harris. I think what I'm going to do first is give your son a call, okay?"

"Oh, you know Jason?"

"Yep, and I have his cell phone number right here. So I'm going to give him a call first and see if he can come help you."

"Oh, okay. That's nice then."

"And if I can't reach him, then I'll send somebody else."

"Okay, because these people need to be dealt with. They need to be told what's what. They need to leave. And there are a lot of them."

"Okay, ma'am. We'll get them out of there one way or another."

23

Communications

In 1971, Albert Mehrabian, a psychology professor at UCLA, published a now-famous study about communication. In it, Dr. M. claims that a huge chunk of communication between human beings is nonverbal. His study posited that about 38 percent of communication is in our tone of voice, and 55 percent is in our body language. That leaves the plain old words we say coming in at a meager 7 percent.

As call-takers, we get only the words and the tone of voice, and if you add the two together, that gives us about 45 percent of the actual message, according to Dr. M. Which probably sounds about right to the cops and paramedics we deal with, who, if asked, would say we get the calls right only about *half of the time*.

Words and tone of voice are all we get, so it's what we work with. We get a lot of background noise too, but since a simple dropped phone can make it sound like a caller is suddenly tumbling down a hundred-foot mine shaft, it's best we don't make assumptions about background noise, either.

"Ma'am, is your husband awake?"

"No!"

"Is he breathing?"

"I don't think so."

"I'm having a hard time hearing you. Can you get all the people in the room to quiet down? Send someone to unlock the door, too. If he's not breathing, we need to start chest compressions."

"It's just me and him."

"What is all the noise?"

"We're watching *How I Met Your Mother*."

"Okay, can you turn that down?"

Technology promises us all sorts of interesting twists and turns in 911. For one thing, many county and city 911 centers now have the capability of receiving emergency text messages. So, take away that 38 percent we get from tone of voice and bring us down to 7 percent. That's not a lot to go on.

And smiley faces don't count as nonverbal, in my opinion. But 911 texting will likely lead to these kinds of things:

"My husband fell on the ice and broke his wrist! ☹"

Or . . .

"Can you send someone over to tell my neighbors to quiet down? ☺ "

Or if shenanigans are suspected . . .

"Can you send someone over to tell my neighbors to quiet down? ;-)"

Also around the corner, or so we hear: 911 by televideo, or Skype, as the kids are calling it these days.

This might actually be helpful. If we can see our callers and get that other precious 55 percent, then maybe we can get a better idea of what the heck is going on. The only problem is that our callers will presumably also be able to see us.

Don't get me wrong, we want all the information we can get. We want full disclosure from our callers. We want the most information possible, so we can save lives. We just don't want to have to look presentable to do it.

One of the biggest benefits of serving the public from behind a phone is that the public never gets to see if I didn't bother to do my hair, or if I'm only running on four hours of sleep (and it looks like less than that), or that I have three empty cans of Diet Sunkist lemonade on my console because taking them to the recycling is *just too much work right now*.

And then there's the very real possibility that some of us will have to start seeing some things we always thought we could avoid by working in dispatch as opposed to in an ambulance. If I haven't made my feelings known about impalements yet, just let me be clear: I am against them. I am also not a fan of vomit, lacerations, severe burns, rashes in undercarriages (or anywhere else for that matter), or boils, on basic principal. And while I've delivered two babies by phone, I have never seen a complete live birth. I understand there are a lot of fluids involved. I'm not a fan of fluids.

At age forty, when I gave blood for the first time, it was such a big deal (because I'm such a pansy) that I wrote a blog post about it. Later that week, a friend who'd read it approached me at a party.

"I was kind of surprised to read that blood makes you so queasy," he smirked. "Given what you do for a living."

"Well, we don't actually see a lot of blood in dispatch." I shrugged. "I mean, unless someone's stolen someone else's Hot Pocket or something." (Then, shit gets real.)

For good or ill, neither texting nor video calling has reached our center yet. So we remain in 45-percent-land with just our ears, our intuition, and past experiences to guide us.

"Okay, Ginny, tell me exactly what happened."

"Well, I just have a little pain in my neck and my arm," says a feeble female voice from somewhere in Wright County.

It seems that the older a caller is, the less he or she wants to admit to feeling badly.

"How old are you?"

"I'm ninety years old this month."

"Are you having any trouble breathing?"

"Well, I guess a little."

It must be generational. I assume she knows it's probably heart-related, or she wouldn't be calling. (Heart attacks in women often manifest as arm, jaw, or neck pain.) But to use her words, it's just a *little* thing. Just a little pain. In her heart—which is just a little important. Her tone is apologetic. She's hoping this isn't interrupting something more important, like perhaps the article about J-Lo I was reading on MSN.com.

"Okay, we're sending someone out to help you, Ginny. While we're on the way, could you please make sure your door is unlocked . . ."

"Oh, please tell them not to use their sirens," she begs. "I don't want the whole neighborhood to hear."

"Well, I'll see what I can do," I tell her.

The siren request usually comes from members of the older generation as well. I think of it as one part "I don't want the neighbors to know my business," two parts "I don't want the neighbors to know I'm old," plus a rounded tablespoon of "I don't want to bother anybody."

The thing is, when I tell the pre-arrival program that I've got a person of a certain age with a certain bunch of symptoms, plus a history of heart problems, it goes into the system as an emergent call, and I have to send the ambulance lights and sirens. I *have* to. It's in the policy manual on page 3,012 or something.

"700 to 732."

"Go ahead."

"732, this is code 3, but the patient is requesting a silent approach."

"But this is a code 3 call?"

"10-4, yes it is."

"So you want us to go code 3 with no sirens?" (Which 732 knows is not allowed.)

"732, just relaying the request." *I don't care if you go code 3 with no pants.* I'm getting approximately 38 percent irritated by 732's tone.

"Copy, 732 responding code 3."

Super. Thanks.

Text might actually be better for transmissions than radio, come to think of it. But who wants to look up from their gurney in the back of an ambulance and see the paramedic busily texting? On second thought . . .

It's not that we don't get along with the responders we dispatch. It's just that despite our best efforts, we are constantly sending them places with only about half of the information that they need or want, and when you're them and not us, it's easy to forget that we are just the messengers. And sometimes the message changes second by second.

"732, you're to access the business in the rear." (I could say "in the back," but I never pass up a chance to say "in the rear." Because I'm twelve years old.)

"732 copied."

"732, apparently the squads now on scene say come to the front, not the rear."

"732, copied, *from the rear.*"

"Copied, 732, you're responding from *the rear.*"

"732, we're not finding anybody. We're going back to the . . . rear."

Please just shoot me in the head. Now. "732, standby one. We'll give county a call back."

"Disregard, 700. We found them."

Oh, for the love.

"It sure is quiet tonight."
  "Don't say the q-word!"
  "Quiet, quiet, quiet."
  "You get the next call. Jerk."

"It's a full moon tonight. God only knows what's going to happen."
  "We'll be able to see the whole moon?"
  "And then shit is going to hit the fan!"
  "Well, then I hope you brought your lucky rabbit foot, or we're hosed."

24

Stella

Stella is prone to singing in dispatch, and loudly. She prefers Christmas carols and doesn't care if you don't. In fact, I think she prefers if you don't.

Most trainees are intimidated by her, at first. She tends to get pretty matter-of-fact when the shit hits the fan. She loves when the shit hits the fan. It's when she does some of her best work.

After four years dispatching cops, I find Stella's matter-of-factness to be downright friendly. Sugary, in fact.

Stella prefers dispatching to call-taking. I prefer call-taking to dispatching. So we're some sort of dispatch yin and yang, apparently. Our best shifts together are the weekend day shifts. Twelve-hour shifts that start at 5:00 or 6:00 A.M. must be peppered with good conversation, or whatever you could call what we did on those shifts.

"So, I've been waiting all morning," Stella might say.

"For me to get less gorgeous? Ain't gonna happen," I might reply.

"For you to rub my cankles."

"Whip your little ham hocks out and let's have a feel."

"You're such a little wenchlette."

"I'm the wenchlette you dream about."

And so on.

My daughter is only a year older than her son, and both children are the most adorable creatures either of us have ever seen, so we spend some of those twelve-hour shifts planning their arranged marriage.

"Does Mariah know she's going to marry my son, or are we just going to surprise her on the day of the ceremony?"

"We'll explain everything to her once we let her out of the trunk."

"Think of the cute babies they're going to make!"

It's quite an honor, actually, that Stella would volunteer her son to marry my daughter. He is her pride and joy, and if dispatching has made me somewhat fearful for Mariah's safety, it causes Stella to downright *obsess* over her son's very life.

When she was in her first year, she took a call of a five-year-old girl choking on a grape. "It was book perfect," she said, meaning the response was *right on*. She acted quickly, her responders were on the scene within minutes, and the patient was whisked to the local ER in record time. Yet she died anyway. So until the day her only child went off to college, Stella never let Tristan eat a single grape without first cutting it in half.

"Jingle Bells" is a favorite of hers, and you never know when she may begin to blurt it out.

~

Stella was dispatching our metro-area paramedics the day a tornado touched down, right in the city.

Tornadoes don't generally visit the Twin Cities proper, and that's good, because there are a lot of people in a very small area.

One minute, she was dispatching our county ambulances at a reasonable pace—a chest pain here, a trouble breathing at the nursing home there—and the next, every ambulance on the screen, plus twenty more we didn't have, was needed code 3. Screens that normally held a dozen or so medicals in various states of en route or arrival were suddenly filled and overflowing into new screens with the more than fifty people who were injured that day.

"I don't remember anything I did that day," she told me later. "I remember somebody saying, 'Hey, did you hear there's a tornado near 694 and 100?' And me saying 'That's like a mile from here!' And then I heard a crackle in my ear. I barely remember anything after that."

The crackle was probably lightning. The tornado was, in fact, less than a mile south of us.

As her call-taker, I remember that Stella didn't move from her chair, take her eyes off her screen, or say a single unnecessary word for about two hours. She calmly and quickly assigned each call to the closest available truck. The calls and their addresses came at her rapid-fire, usually sent by me, and as the number of trucks slowly doubled and more crews came in to help, she used her fifteen years of geographical knowledge to send the closest trucks to each. It's a bit like playing a game of memory with a gun to your head.

"I remember one thing," she said. "I realized too late at one point that I accidentally crossed trucks." Crossing trucks means miscalculating the distance or route to a call, and causing a truck to literally pass the closer truck along the way. In this small area, it probably meant a delay of a minute or two, and the patient was not critically injured. Yet . . .

"I thought about that for days," she said, still kicking herself two years later. "I couldn't watch any of the news footage afterward. I couldn't talk about it. That's what I remember."

I suppose that's what makes a good dispatcher, though. Relentless self-criticism and the inability to pat oneself on the back, lest it make you complacent.

"I don't remember anything but you kicking that tornado's ass," I told her later.

"It's embarrassing how much you worship me."

"And I remember somebody asking if we were supposed to take cover. And me laughing. And then thinking that I really didn't want to die in this dispatch center. Or any other dispatch center."

"Amen, sister girl."

Stella had a real adjustment to make when her son went off to college. Luckily, my kid went away one year earlier.

"How's my future daughter-in-law doing?"

"I never hear from her. Potentially kidnapped by a terrorist group, or joined the circus."

"Well, if you ever see her again, tell her that her crazy future mother-in-law says 'hi.'"

"We're doing another group lottery thing. The jackpot is at $240 million. You in?"

"I don't have any cash."

"You're going to be really sad when we all quit and there's nobody but you answering calls and dispatching and the whole county goes to shit."

"Borrow me a dollar?"

"Guess so."

"You're a lifesaver."

"See you at the press conference."

25

Stayin' Alive

Dispatch is not the place to start a long story. You will get interrupted. Starting a long story is a lot like saying, "Isn't it quiet in here?" It's flat-out asking for trouble.

Yet, we try.

"So, I'm jogging along, and even kind of enjoying it . . ." I say to Stella during a break in the action. (She and I are training for a half-marathon.)

"And you were thinking about how great I look in my new running pants . . ."

"Yes, of course," I continue. "And then I hear this dog bark from a distance, and I'm like 'Where's the cute puppy?' And next thing I know . . ."

Riiiiiinnnnnnng.

We each have certain phone lines assigned to us, depending on the position we are sitting in during the shift. This particular line is Stella's. So I have to shut up because she's the only person who appears to care about my puppy story.

Stella holds up a finger.

"Stand by," she says gravely. "I have to save a life."

It's a non-emergent line. So, not likely. It's just something we like to say. Partially to be cute. Partially because between non-emergent transfers, migraine headaches, policy changes, false alarms, and everything else we do that's less like watching *Grey's Anatomy* and more like watching C-SPAN, we are generally in tune with how very little we actually get to save lives.

Though it happened long enough ago that I never even worked with the guy, my coworkers still get a bang out of recounting the night when John (not his real name), a highly excitable and fairly new EMD, picked up the phone to a cardiac arrest in progress. Stories differ on what it was that made this particular call seem so rife with lifesaving possibility, but John entered the call, stood triumphantly (sending his rolling chair flying behind him), and exclaimed, "Ma'am, I'm going to tell you how to save his life!"

Nobody seems to remember if he did save a life. If not, it wasn't for lack of enthusiasm.

Anyway, I won't get to finish my jogging story for another half an hour because instead of saving a life, Stella must spend the next thirty minutes trying to locate a wallet that a patient says he left in one of our ambulances. Five phone calls and three supervisors later, the patient calls back to tell her he found his wallet at home. It's a glamorous life.

At this point, my jogging story will be fairly anticlimactic because a) it's not much of a story, and b) all it really had going for it was the glib way I was trying to tell it and Stella's comic interruptions. The fact that I sprained my ankle rubbernecking at a cute dog just isn't that noteworthy. It sure isn't as important as saving a life.

For most life-saves, we would need a time machine, because we are too late for the save. The found husband is a body and not a husband anymore. The accident has happened. The shot has been fired. The blood has been bled. The short minutes of possibility are past. The window closed.

It doesn't mean we don't try. We always try. It only means that in most cases, everybody can do everything right, and everything still isn't enough.

"Hi, Betty? Tell me exactly what happened."

"I don't know. I just found him on the toilet. He's not moving."

"Is he conscious?"

"Honey! Honey? No."

"Is he breathing?"

"I don't know. Russell! He's really pale. He's . . . blue."

"Do you think that he's beyond help?"

This is the big question. It's the difference between trying to save Russell or not. If she can't tell me for sure that he's gone, then we have to try. I can't see him. I can give her clues: is he cold and stiff in a warm environment? Is this an expected death? But I can't call it for her. How blue is too blue? She has to be the one to decide. Most people aren't ready to make that call. How could they be?

"I don't know. I don't know!"

Okay, Betty. Here we go.

"Can you get him on the floor?"

"I don't think so. I'd hurt him. He's so big."

"Okay, we're not worried about hurting him as much as just getting his heart going. We need to start chest compressions."

"Oh my God. I don't think . . ."

"Ma'am, let's try. Let's get him flat on his back."

"Okay. I'll try."

"Then come right back to the phone."

Betty sets down the phone, and I'm powerless. At this point, some people never come back to the phone. They either freelance the CPR or they get hysterical and run around freaking out until the cops arrive. I hate sending callers away from the phone, but it had to be done. It's hard enough to save a blue man, and darn near impossible to save a blue man on the toilet.

Incidentally, from my very skewed world view, using the toilet is an extremely dangerous activity, tantamount to bungee jumping, attempting to summit Everest, or taking medical advice from any one of Oprah's "doctors." I've taken so many dead-on-the-toilet calls that every time I'm on the throne anymore, I wonder if this will be the fatal sitting.

After two long minutes and many grunts and groans, Betty actually gets Russell to the floor. She returns, panting and excited. We both are. We feel the possibility.

"Okay, Betty. I want you to put the heel of one hand between the nipples, the other hand on top of that."

At this point, I don't need the script in front of me. I know the song by heart.

"I want you to pump hard and fast four hundred times or until help arrives. Count out loud so we can count together."

Now I become like a demented marching band instructor yelling to the beat. The goal is to keep Betty pumping fast enough to make a difference. To keep the rhythm going until someone else can take over.

"Faster, Betty! ONE and TWO and THREE and FOUR and . . ."

If you ever find yourself in Betty's position (and I sure hope that you don't), think of the song "Stayin' Alive" by the Bee Gees. That's how fast you need to pump, about a hundred beats per minute. No joke. Love it or hate it, '70s disco can save lives.

Ah, hah, hah, hah, stayin' alive, stayin' alive. Ah, hah, hah, hah, stayin' aliiiiiiiive!!

The Queen classic "Another One Bites the Dust" also works, tempo-wise. But I can't recommend that one.

Betty and I count and pump, count and pump. We reach one hundred. She pants heavily. "I don't think this is helping," she says.

"Betty, do you think that he is beyond help?" Because I think that he is.

"I don't know."

"Let's tilt his head back and lift his chin and listen for breathing."

"Okay."

"Is he breathing?"

"I don't know."

Then I don't know; so we keep going.

Stayin' alive, stayin' alive.

I wish I could tell you something good here. Like, Betty was wrong and her husband was actually more white than blue. Like there was a spark left, and Betty and I kept it going just long enough. I wish I could say that the medics arrived, hooked up a defibrillator, and recharged Russell. And that they took him to the hospital and he went home two days later.

Instead, an officer arrived to a dead man on his bathroom floor, immediately saw what Betty and I couldn't, and canceled the ambulance.

I stay on the phone for the crying. It seems wrong to disconnect from it. Plus, I need a minute before the next call. Sixty seconds for grief. I hope that someone is touching Betty, somehow. A hand on her shoulder. An arm around her. I wish it could be me. I would tell her she did a great job.

Somewhere, there is a woman named Betty with whom I tried to save a life. There are many, many Bettys. We might pass each other in a shopping mall or speak again on the phone, but we will never know.

~

And sometimes we don't save a life because it didn't need saving. Sometimes the baby who was choking was actually the baby who was gurgling. Sometimes the uncle not breathing in his La-Z-Boy is actually the uncle who just looks really scary when he falls asleep sitting up. We are only as informed as our callers. Sometimes that's . . . not very.

"I need an ambulance for my girlfriend!"

"Tell me exactly what happened."

"I think she drank too much. She's not breathing. I don't know what's going on."

"Sir, if she's not breathing, we need to start chest compressions. Is that the case? She's not breathing?"

"Right!"

"Lift her chin and tilt her head back. Put your ear to her mouth. Can you feel or hear any breathing?"

"I don't think so."

"Okay, I want you to put the heel of one hand between the nipples and put your other hand over that . . ."

And we are off on our chest-compression journey. We're pumping. We're counting. We're stayin' alive. We're . . .

"What the fuck are you doing to me?"

"Uh."

"John? What was that?"

"She's awake. Uh. She's awake, yeah."

"Are you trying to fucking kill me?"

Poor John. That might be the last he sees of those nipples for a while.

~

Still, I am the proud holder of a Lifesaver Pin. Most of my fellow dispatchers have them as well. Joe's security badge is peppered with them, like little decorative bullets.

I'd like to think that if I ever need to save a life in person, I already know all the moves by heart. But if I should somehow forget, I know the number to call for the best demented marching-band instructors you could ever imagine. Even (especially) Joe, who routinely calls me a harelip dog. (I don't know what that is, but I'm too afraid to Google it.)

My life-save was a successful Heimlich maneuver. By the time I took that call, I had given those same instructions probably fifty times. But this time, there was still a spark. It doesn't mean I'm such a great dispatcher. It doesn't mean I'm not. It just means that everybody involved did everything right. And this time, everybody and everything was enough.

DISPATCHER: "Have you ever had a stroke before?"
WIFE: "Yeah, I had a stroke a couple years ago."
HUSBAND (NEXT TO HER): "WHERE THE HELL WAS I?"

26

Missing Things

I open my e-mail to find a note from Danielle, and the subject line reads: "Don't be mad at me."

Oh, dear.

Danielle is a few years younger than me, but has a few years more of seniority. We don't see eye to eye on some things. Plus, while I was taught to introduce negative statements with gentle words like "Sometimes I have observed" and "This is just my perspective, but," Danielle dwells in a world that is more absolute.

Caroline—

I don't like to be the one to say this, but you need to pay attention better, and stop missing stuff. You are going to get all of our computers, etc., taken away. If that happens, people will be really pissed. Someone has already complained about you.

Well, oh. Oh, shit.

And hell yeah, I'm mad. Because it's all true. A hundred percent spot-on.

If you've ever done shift work, perhaps you've heard the term "double back." I don't know if this applies to all dispatch centers, but to us, it means to work the night shift, get off around 5:00 or 6:00 A.M., then come back after a short break of only eight or nine hours.

I was routinely getting off from a twelve-hour shift at 5:00 A.M., then doubling back for an eight-hour 2:00 P.M. shift. And I was really sucking at it. I was reporting to work on four or five hours of sleep, and it was shitty, fretful, *nervous that I was going to oversleep* sleep.

On receipt of this note, I was as tired as usual, so my response took a few rough incarnations before it was send-ready.

Dear Danielle, You look really fat in those ambulance pants lately. Yes, I realize that you're 6 months pregnant.

Dear Danielle, It's not my fault. Also, you're not the boss of me.

Dear Danielle, This is where I'd like to point out a mistake you've made, but nothing is really coming to mind. Fuck.

Dear Danielle, I'm not mad. I'm glad you were brave enough to say something. I'm using my laptop to keep myself awake, and you're right . . . I'm missing things.

Sigh.

Shit.

What sorts of things?

For example, we have more than a dozen different outstate channels to monitor, and as the air-ambulance dispatcher, my primary responsibility is to answer the channel dedicated to the helicopters. But their voices are blending in with the other channels for me. I'm missing them. Pilots are calling me, and it's not getting through the fog.

Dangerous.

People like Danielle *are* hearing them, thankfully, and picking up my slack.

Another responsibility we all have: when we send a crew on a call, we need to move coverage. For example, if I send one town's ambulance to a call, either I need to make sure there is another crew available in that same town or I need to have an ambulance from a nearby town stage in between the two, in case another call comes in.

I'm forgetting.

Tonight on Channel 5 Eyewitness News: *911 Dispatchers: Asleep at the Wheel!*

Danielle's note scares the hell out of me, but that doesn't make it any easier to sleep during the day than it was before. In fact, the added pressure makes sleep that much more difficult.

I hunt down two sets of blackout shades for my bedroom. It's not enough just to mount them on the curtain rods, because the sun peeks through on all sides. I purchase rolls and rolls of Velcro strips, cut the blackout shades to fit the windows, and cover each window. Jim, who routinely works until 2:00 A.M., notes that sun still seeps through the blackout shades, so he purchases several rolls of black duct tape and covers the blackout shades completely with strip after strip.

We essentially duct-tape our bedroom into darkness.

Benadryl gelcaps become my little pink best friends.

I start seeking out Internet advice as to how to start winning at the night shift. WebMD tells me to stop drinking caffeinated beverages toward the end of my shift. (This is when I generally begin to slam coffee and Diet Coke out of desperation.) I am also advised to be "sleep savvy" and plan my sleep. WebMD also tells me all of the things that the night shift can cause, such as cardiovascular disease, diabetes, obesity, stomach problems, ulcers, depression, and an increased risk of injuries and accidents.

I once went to the Internet because my ears were ringing. The Internet told me I might have cancer. You'd think I'd learn not to ask the Internet about anything health related. But the good news is that my newfound fear of cardiovascular disease, ulcers, and accidents has me fully alert and frightened as hell at the tender hour of 3:00 A.M.

I chortle out loud when I reach the part where WebMD advises me to talk to my manager about switching out of night shifts if I am having trouble.

I find another site with advice about "turnarounds." If I insist on switching from night shifts to day hours, I am told to nap from about 10:00 A.M. to 2:00 P.M., then just "potter around" for the evening. Also, eat carbs and crackers whilst pottering. I don't know what this means. It sounds British.

I come to the conclusion that what I'm doing isn't healthy, but it's for a good cause. I petition management to get rid of my shifts with the tight turnaround.

"We'll see what we can do."

My next shift with Danielle, I'm on high alert. It's not that I got more sleep, just that I have more fear. I jump at every ringing phone. Every crew gets answered almost before they finish their radio traffic. I am a top-flight partner! An eager beaver. I am mostly awake!

I hope I can make it last.

"The ambulance will be there shortly, ma'am."
"Who's coming? Is it you?"
"No, I'm sending two paramedics over to help you."
"Oh, too bad. You sound very nice."

27

Jurassic Park

Joe enters the dispatch center at 1:50 P.M. and takes it all in.

"I must be in Jurassic Park," he announces. "Because there's nothing but dinosaurs in here."

In truth, there is an even mix of, ahem, older dispatchers and younger ones. Joe has begun dating a smoking-hot EMT from an outstate company, and so he probably feels pretty young, but he is about my age. I lack seniority, but I am slowly becoming one of the older ones. I am darn near forty. Half of the paramedics I am sending on calls have never seen a rotary phone.

We are all ages, but we be tight. We talk about our spouses, we talk about our exes. We either love the Vikings or feel sorry for those of us who love the Vikings. We love each other enough to avoid politics (most of the time).

Carl, one of the dinosaurs, sends a glance Joe's way and sniffs. "Did you hear something?" he asks me.

"I sure didn't hear Joe calling you a prehistoric creature," I reply.

"Me neither."

I could be a dinosaur one day. In dispatch, as in many jobs, you can either spend your career as a worker bee or you can try to make your way up the management ladder. Managers have a tough gig. If a manager is hired from outside an agency, he is the jerk-face that they hired instead of choosing someone from within. What's wrong with one of us? Why would they do that? Who the hell is this guy? And now we have to train him on our policies? *Screw that!*

If a manager is hired from within, he becomes a traitor. Not at first, but slowly. At first we are *so happy* for him. But then we realize he's not one of us anymore. He is acting all . . . managerial. Managers have to tell us depressing things about the schedule. They have to talk to us when we call in sick too much. They say things like, "Gottaminute?" and then we have to sit with them in an office and hear recordings of our phone or radio fuckups. Then we have to try to remember exactly what was going on in the room, on the phone, and on the radio that caused us to make that decision, say that thing, make that call. And we never know, because there are so many calls. And after a certain number of years, they all start to blend together, and doesn't he know this? And why is he asking me these questions?

Managers have to answer when we page them with techie problems at 3:00 A.M., but they also aren't allowed to complain about their Monday-through-Friday schedules in our presence. They have to limp our old technology along, apologizing for the lack of funds to buy us new equipment. They have to convince us that it's acceptable that the teenagers at the Culver's drive-through wear higher quality headsets than we do.

"Oh, he used to be a great guy, but now he's drinking the company Kool-Aid," someone might say after a particularly brutal or truthful gottaminute.

I am using the pronoun "he" in these scenarios because I've only met one female supervisor along this path, and it's been twelve years, and she wasn't our direct supervisor. I can't tell you why any other female might shy away from management, but I can tell you why *this* female has.

Because I hate conflict.

Oh, conflict between other people is fine. I can listen to that all day on the job, and have. But to be the cause of someone's conflict? To be the giver of a "gottaminute"? I would rather take ten thousand ingrown-toenail calls.

Which leaves me with my second option as a dispatcher. To remain a dispatcher. Forever. For thirty years. Which is forever. To take the toenail calls, the back-pain calls, the children-who-don't-live calls, the drills, the calls we wish were drills. To work night shift until I'm so old I don't need day shift. To become a dinosaur. To ask permission to pee. Forever.

"Carl," I say with authority I don't have. "I'm stepping out to use the biff."

"Permission to step out denied."

"Sheesh," I sigh dramatically. "I can't work in these conditions."

The dinosaur lifts his head and grins. "Are there any conditions in which you *can* work?"

"Tell me exactly what happened."

"Exactly what happened? Well, there was a tree stand and there was my drunk friend, Mark. And they're not together anymore."

28

Babies

"Hello? Tell me exactly what hap . . ."

"Listen. My wife, she's been having contractions, and last time . . . well, she darn near sneezed and out come the baby. So, you know . . ."

"How far along is she?"

"She's ready, you know? I don't know. Eight months? Nine months? But she's ready."

"Is that her . . ."

"Yeah, she screamin'."

"Can you see any part of the baby's head right now?"

"What did you say?"

"Can you see any part of the baby?"

"She got her pants on. I don't want to see that."

"Aren't you her . . . husband?"

"Sure as hell."

"Then . . ."

"Baby, they're sending an ambulance. It's all right. You're sendin' somebody, right?"

"They are on the way. Sir, how far apart are the contractions?"

"I don't know. A minute."

"How many other children has she had?"

"By me?"

"Altogether."

"All what?"

"How many kids does she have?"

"Five."

"Yeah, she needs to get her pants off, sir. Like, *right now*."

My patient was scoring something like four out of five in the pre-arrival questions for "imminent birth," so I was getting kind of excited. I was praying for that one big imminent sneeze.

And then the darned ambulance arrived.

"They're here, ma'am. And we're good. She's got her pants off now."

"Okay, sir, thank you. You can disconnect."

Delivering a baby by phone is just about the most fun you can have with a headset on, but it's a rare thing. We get a lot of *almost a baby* calls, but precious few of them end with a crying newborn on the other end of the line. It's not that the births themselves go wrong, it's that the darned police or medics show up and start helping, and all we get is a "thanks" or, more commonly, a click. In twelve years, I've had two complete deliveries. I waited six years for the first one. It happened on a December 31, technically New Year's Eve, around 4:00 A.M.

"Sir, tell me exactly . . ."

"My wife's having contractions!"

"Okay, how far along is she?"

If we assist the caller from before the delivery until somewhere around wrapping the umbilical cord, we are eligible for baby bragging rights in the form of a "Stork Pin." The Stork Pin is exactly what it sounds like. It's a decorative stick pin we can attach to our uniform sweaters featuring an animated stork. Bragging rights. *How many storks do you have?* Blue stork for boys, pink stork for girls.

"Sir, can you see any part of the baby right now?"

"Ahhhhhhhhhgggg!!!"

"You didn't hear the question, did you, sir?"

"No, ma'am."

"It's okay. We're coming."

It's not like my involvement is so critical. I tell him not to let her sit on the toilet. I tell him several other things he doesn't hear because his wife is feeling the full force of her contractions. No matter, really. It's not like babies don't just come unbidden, and regardless of who's on the phone or what is being said. This baby is no exception. This baby is completely running the show, and I am one of three cheerleaders waving my pompons wildly until he comes out.

And when he does, I am *high*.

"Is that your first baby?" Mira stands up in her half cube to address me with a huge grin.

"It is!"

"Boy or girl?"

"I don't know!"

"You didn't ask?"

"Dad was a touch busy."

One of the responding medics calls and says, "It's a boy!" He is happy largely because the birth didn't take place inside his ambulance.

But, it's a big win for the dispatch center.

Plus, I get a blue pin.

~

Shortly after my nephew, Eric, was born, a young man called my partner to tell us that he had awoken to find his infant son dead on the couch next to him. Under him, possibly. He didn't know. I dispatched the ambulance. My partner kept him on the phone and tried to understand his casual attitude. He apparently just *wasn't upset* about this development. Can we help the baby? Start CPR? *Don't think so*, he says. Don't think so?

I dispatched it as a "baby not breathing" call. We must always have a way not to say "dead." We certainly won't put that word with "baby." To start with, we're not there. So we don't know death with

166 / Tell Me Exactly What Happened

any real certainty. More importantly, not breathing feels reversible. A human can stop breathing, then start breathing. We let the paramedics determine whether it's reversible. We wait and we hope for the best.

Don't think so, he says.

A few minutes after the ambulance arrives, we listen as one of the medics calls an ER doctor on a lower channel, as they often do. It is about the baby, and the baby is gone.

We are heartbroken. Mothers, fathers, dispatchers.

"Who puts a baby on a couch with him, then falls asleep?" someone says. We play the call back to analyze his tone. It doesn't matter. The baby was gone when he called us. Suffocated. Powerless, like us. The police will decide whether it's suspicious. It doesn't matter what we think about it. I tried not to think about it, and did a decent job of that. But then I saw my newborn nephew.

My brother's son, Eric, was born in the summer. He is fair and light-haired like my sister-in-law. Serious and stubborn like my brother. Blue eyes. I met him when he was twenty-four hours old. Since my own daughter is adopted, this was the first time I'd held such a brand-new, fragile human. Suddenly, all the babies I'd been hearing about on the phone had a face. Babies are born, but some babies die. What if I got attached to this one? What could happen? I didn't hold him much those first few months. He felt too heavy. It felt like too much to carry.

Instead, standing with my sister-in-law in her dining room, I tried to talk to her about baby CPR. Was she certified? Did she know what to do? Push on the breastbone with your two peace fingers, not your whole hand. She must have thought I was such a jerk. Or crazy. She promised she knew what she needed to know.

As Eric got older, and less vulnerable, I got more comfortable. I watched him break free of a swaddle. I watched him knock into things, pick himself up. He'd learned the difference between hot and cold. He is not made of spun sugar; he is a normal boy.

The more difficult thing to admit is that I just got used to baby-not-breathing calls. You can get used to things. To the point that you forget things you never imagined you could forget. A friend may ask me, "Anything exciting happen at work today?" and sometimes I am hard-pressed to answer. The most honest answer is "Probably." But the details don't always stick anymore. It's not that the calls stop mattering; it's that they begin to cancel each other out. One is similar to the other, which is similar to three more. I figure it's a numbers thing. Call after call after call. Generally, the forgetting part is a mercy.

Except regarding the stork-pin calls.

Two babies *born on the phone* out of how many thousands of calls I have answered in twelve years?

I wish I could say more about my second stork pin, but all I know is that it is pink. I wear it proudly on my uniform sweater, and despite the numbers, I hope that every next ring is a *new baby breathing* call.

DISPATCHER: "So, just so I understand. The patient has an eight-inch turkey baster in her nose?"

CALL-TAKER: "Yep. I don't get it. It's not even Thanksgiving."

DISPATCHER: "How old?"

CALL-TAKER: "It's in the notes! Why?"

DISPATCHER: "I'm just trying to get a picture in my mind."

CALL-TAKER: "No pictures. That's the great thing about dispatching. We don't have to see this shit."

29

Gottaminute

"Gottaminute?"

I have just arrived and am getting ready to answer metro 911 calls for the next twelve hours. So, yes. I have a lot of minutes, and can spare at least a couple for Norm.

Norm is the boss.

If this is the first time you're meeting him, it's because I don't see him much. Managers work during the day, often leaving by 3:00 P.M. or 4:00 P.M., and that's generally when my fun is just beginning.

Norm has a tough gig. He's a technical guy who loves to problem solve. Unfortunately, half or more of the problems he's charged with solving aren't technical problems, but people problems. Conflict, personalities, misunderstandings. None of these things can be solved by writing the right macro, finding the faulty wire, or rebooting the hard drive.

"Did you hear what 710 just said to me on the radio, Norm?"

"Nope."

"He's been giving me attitude ever since he went on duty."

"That's your *perception*," Norm says. That is what he always says. And then he might walk off and start talking to himself. Actually, he is talking into a Bluetooth device, but until I realized that, I totally *perceived* that he was talking to himself.

I follow Norm to his office. *Gottaminutes*, as we call them, are rarely good. Norm has never called me to his office to tell me what an awesome job I'm doing. That's not his fault; it's just not generally done. It's not necessary, and there's no time for that. We're in the business of putting out fires. If you don't put out a fire, it stays a fire. Put it out correctly; that's your job. If you don't put out the fire correctly, you get a *gottaminute*.

Sometimes it's a question: *Was there a fuckup? Let's listen to the recordings. Tell me what you were thinking here.*

Sometimes it's a fact: *There was a fuckup. Let's listen to the recordings and you can tell me why the hell you fucked this up.*

Norm shuts his office door. This is totally unnecessary, since his office is already closed off from the dispatch center as well as the outer hallway.

Indications are that I might have fucked up.

I mine the memory banks, but nothing comes to mind. Usually, if something goes wonky with a call, or if a wrong address gets entered, or I fail to send the closest truck, I send an e-mail to Norm so he doesn't get blindsided by it. Better that he hear it from me before he hears it from a sergeant from one of the counties we serve or a firefighter from a scene halfway across the state.

He gestures for me to sit. His face is a fire I'm pretty sure I started and failed to put out correctly.

"So, you have been posting on Facebook when you're supposed to be working."

Well, *oh.*

Oh.

Yes. But.

What?

I had. I wasn't the only one, but yes. I had been posting, writing, tinkering on my laptop in there for years.

For the next few minutes, Norm detailed my most egregious offenses, to include posting a picture of myself and a coworker with our work boots up on the counter, and another picture of a coworker dressed up for St. Patrick's Day, which was innocent enough but for the careless inclusion of the monitors behind her. The monitors contained addresses and the nature of the calls at those addresses.

And more.

And then another thing.

I had been posting about the job to relieve stress and to entertain, and out of boredom during downtimes, and I had been in violation without knowing it. Or maybe I didn't want to know.

I had royally fucked up.

The verdict: Guilty. The punishment? I can't have nice things.

In order to stay awake, stay engaged, fight boredom, we bring things with us to dispatch. I can no longer bring those things.

Suddenly, all of the little lifeboats that a dispatcher might use to keep afloat in a sea of waiting . . . books, magazines, laptops, cell phones, knitting . . . forbidden. Not for three months, not for a year. Forever. Till death or termination.

Full disclosure: I don't knit. But I wanted to. Never more so than in that moment.

I was shaking when I got back to my console.

"You can take all that stuff out to your car," Norm said in a low voice, gesturing to all my precious downtime toys.

"Even my phone?"

"Yes, your phone."

I felt ten years old.

I checked the clock.

Eleven hours and forty-one minutes left of this shift.

I had failed my profession, my boss, and my callers. Yet, in that moment, I was panicking about my phone. My computer. My books. All of the things that made the in-between times bearable. The act of surfing, shopping, comparing, reading—checking the heck out.

It doesn't occur to me that if checking out of the dispatch center matters so much, that if being in the moment is so painful, that maybe I need to change the moments I am living in. I'm not concerned even one bit about how I'd made the department look or how I'd made Norm look. It is *just so unfair*.

I skulk out to my car, somewhat panicked about the idea of leaving these things there to be stolen. My years in police dispatch have made me hyperaware that sometimes valuables are taken from cars. From my perspective, *all the time*.

I return to my console and stare at the screens. My eyes burn with tears.

I punish Norm by not saying a word to him, all day. He seems not to notice even one whit. At some point I think he's talking to me, and I am eager to ignore him. Then I realize he's talking into his Bluetooth again. I look around the room, at my cohorts, trying to decipher if anyone else is being punished so dramatically. Rick cradles a crossword puzzle. Alicia stares intently at her smartphone. Everyone else has a laptop open. I appear to be the only dispatcher of this particular bunch who is in the penalty box.

I throw an eleven-hour, forty-one-minute pity party.

And that day, I start leaving 911.

"Anything to pass down from the night shift?"

"Well, yeah."

"Really? Is there a call on hold or something?"

"Hah. No. But there's this guy, and he's looking for his mom, who maybe was airlifted from Princeton, but he's not sure, and she's missing her purse, and it has her medications in it, and her rosary . . ."

"No, no. I'm not taking that Charlie Foxtrot. Give it to someone who was already here."

"Charlie Fox-what?"

"Cluster Fu-"

"*Oh.* Copy."

30

Leaving 911

But of course, I can't just leave.

After eleven years on the job, I know there are other 911 centers I could work for. Heck, I know most of their non-emergent phone numbers by heart. There are *always* other 911 centers. And they generally all pay better than a reporter's salary and less than a cop's salary. They all promise better hours once you've been there a while, and none can say how long a while is. They all have their own policies, their own quirks, their divas, their saints, and their assholes.

I would start at the bottom of the seniority totem pole wherever I went, which would mean returning to the scheduling gutter for the fourth time. I would have to learn a new set of policies and personalities, a fourth time.

Nope.

I decide instead to go into technical writing. It's a good, sturdy career that involves writing about very boring, benign topics like software or machinery or how to assemble a bunk bed. If done correctly, there is very little death or dismemberment in the field of technical writing. This is appealing.

I'll keep dispatching so that I can eat, but after work I learn how to write things like instructions, technical manuals, and all manner of writing that would put any night-shifter right to sleep. I buy a book called *Technical Writing for Dummies* and wish like hell I could read it at work. I enroll in an online technical-writing class. I will eventually need to do a couple of free internships to prove myself. This is going to take a little time. Like a year or more.

At twenty-eight hours a week, fifty-two weeks a year, that means at least another 1,456 hours in dispatch. That's a lot of hours without my fun downtime toys.

As long as I'm stuck there, I decide to take an interest in my job. What else can I do?

I become hypervigilant as a defense mechanism. And not just over my own trucks, calls, and dispatches, but over everyone else's as well.

"Natalie, did you call the hospital on that ship going to Regions?" *I know she didn't. I've been watching her like a hawk. A hawk without a laptop.*

"Oh! No, I will."

"Let me grab that for ya." *Please. Because I'm bored to death and none of my trucks are even moving.*

I ride a line between being genuinely helpful and being over-helpy Miss Helperton. Meanwhile, I hope that nobody asks why I don't bring anything in anymore.

One good thing about all of this: It's super easy to pack for work now.

Lunch? Check. Purse? Check. Coffee mug? *Duh.*

In dispatch, we tend to have *bag ladies*. Bag ladies don't have to be ladies, they just have to be anyone who brings in enough bags on any given shift to appear as though ready for either a long trip abroad or the zombie apocalypse. Between my laptop, twelve hours' worth of snacks, a book, the Sunday paper, a stack of bills, my makeup bag (in case of fabled Skype dispatching or cute sit-along), my Tums (in case of Culver's), my Advil (in case of headache or zombie apocalypse), I was rounding the corner toward bag-lady status.

But not anymore! I travel light as a feather. It's somewhat freeing, though I would never tell Norm that.

I spend long minutes at a time watching trucks and helicopters go from point A to point B on the GPS map. I ponder whether this route or that was the best way to go. I check and recheck addresses.

Each of us is assigned certain lines to pick up in order to distribute the workload evenly. When someone else's line lights up, I sit up, and wait. I wait for them to miss it. I hope he doesn't hear it, or that she's too busy—so I can grab it.

I look forward to callers' long, involved stories. Tell me exactly what happened, sir. *Start on the day you were born.*

I welcome the Charlie Foxtrot.

I become a volunteer *shit magnet.*

One day, as I'm sifting through the policy and procedure manual trying to find the answer to a question that is not actually my problem, an idea hits me. The policy manual, written by half a dozen different people and edited by no one, features sloppy grammar, inconsistent bullet points, run-on sentences, sentence fragments, and multiple crimes against commas. *This thing is awful.* Someone should revise *the whole thing.*

Who else but bored-stiff, wannabe-technical-writer girl should do this? Nobody, that's who. I beg Norm to let me revise the policy manual. He happily agrees. I figure this will eat up my downtime for at least a month or two. I stretch it out to three months.

I resist the urge to plant little *Waldos* throughout the book to see who's paying attention. Like: "If the backup crew is not at quarters, alpha page them to come in. If they don't respond in five minutes, send out a second page. If they don't respond to the second page, *release the flying monkeys.*"

Or: "Incoming calls are to be answered on the first or second ring. It answers before third ring or *else it gets the hose again.*"

It is so hard to be good.

It frequently occurs to me that I am actually proving a point that Norm often makes about whether he should allow any of us to have downtime toys. Judging by this experiment, I am clearly a better, more attentive dispatcher without them. When I was farting around on my computer all shift long, I was running the risk of getting downtime toys taken away from everyone. Now that I'm a model worker, I could very well be running the risk of getting downtime toys taken away from everyone.

But I know better. I'm a better dispatcher because I know I am leaving.

Every boring hospital-to-hospital transfer I take now is just one less I will have to do. Every injured child, every screaming wife, every vague address, and every DOA is just one less that I will have to take. I see the tunnel and the light, and when I get there, I'll be able to cut my strings, pee when I want to, and sleep at night just like a real girl.

I see in my coworkers the enthusiasm that I lack.

There's Gordy, who can recite full paragraphs of the policy manual from memory. There's Stella, who can work a tornado from start to finish and only cross trucks *one freaking time*. There's Richard, who can dispatch a helicopter just from eavesdropping on a call-taker who doesn't even know it's needed yet. There's Mona, who still has total compassion after forty years.

These are the people who should be doing this job. Time for me to just be one of the many who are grateful that they are.

"Tell me exactly what happened."

"My husband just stuck his hand in the snowblower, and he lost a finger!"

"Okay, we'll get someone started. Do you have the finger?"

"Can they do something with that?"

"Yes, sometimes they can. You'll want to put it in a clean plastic bag."

"Oh, God. Okay. I'll go find my husband's . . . finger. It's not supposed to snow in April."

"I agree, ma'am. It's really not."

31

The Last Day

On my last day, a sixteen-year-old girl committed suicide.

Summer in Minnesota is something we all crave for months. The change usually happens fast, from winter to a brief spring, then next thing you know, you're swatting mosquitoes and standing in line for soft-serve and wondering why you always forget the sunscreen until it's too late. And with the sun come the outdoor sports, the long hikes, the off-leash dogs, the heat exposure, the heated arguments, the restlessness and anger so much more fluid and ready and ignitable.

But I don't know why that young girl killed herself.

I've thought of suicide many times, but I lack commitment. And after almost thirty-five years of thinking about it, I also feel pretty strongly that I don't really want to. I just hate pain. And sometimes, life is pain. And then it's good. And then it's not. And I wish I could rely on the good parts, but I can't, so I throw up my hands and think about ending it. Then I realize I just need a nap. I'm not making light of it. This is actually and truly how my mind works and the circles it goes around while chasing its own tail.

I've learned, through therapy and through experience, that I'm an addictive personality who is prone to fits of anxiety and depression. I treat these maladies with regular counseling and good self care. They are as real as any disease, they can be deadly, and they require my attention daily.

It's hard to admit to these things. But it's impossible not to, knowing that admitting them may help another person feel less alone. And when I'm out in the world and I see a Hawaiian shirt and I'm reminded of Mack, I can at least know that anything I hid from him when he was suffering is no longer hidden to anyone else who might need to know me. I am truly an open book now.

I wish that girl had called me. Isn't that just so vain?

Tell me exactly what happened.

Like I could have said something so profound. Like I have any idea what she must have been going through in order to do what she did. But maybe. That's both the great promise and the great torture of being the *first* first responder. The possibility of saving a life.

Maybe I could have told her what my therapist told me: that when someone commits suicide, the ripple is so great as to affect hundreds and thousands of people. Maybe I could have told her that the things she wanted so desperately not to deal with that day would barely register on her radar in a year. Would she even remember them at seventeen? I could have told her to imagine the people she loved the most finding her, grieving her, blaming themselves, and agonizing for the rest of their lives. Maybe I would have said the exact wrong thing. Maybe I would have made it worse. No. What could be worse than what happened?

Sixteen. It could have been a boyfriend. It could have been a Facebook post. A D-minus in chemistry. Or it could have been something more painful than I can imagine.

She didn't call me or any 911 call-taker that day.

Her mother called 911 upon finding her. She had used a gun.

I had her mom on the phone for only about a minute. I tried to find out if the girl was still breathing. She couldn't tell, and of course she was under way too much stress to answer many questions.

But she thought maybe her daughter was breathing. I think for a few moments we both wanted her daughter to be breathing so badly that we let ourselves believe it.

"732, take a code 3 in Round Lake, on a sixteen-year-old with a self-inflicted gunshot wound at ABC Road."

A sixteen-year-old *girl* with a self-inflicted gunshot wound. This is not a call we take every day. Sixteen-year-old girls don't often have access to guns. But more than that, it's just not a route they normally take. They lack commitment. They want to be heard or noticed. They don't necessarily want to end it, so they take pills or make superficial cuts.

Mom disconnected, and I tried to call her back.

"Hi! You've reached . . ." I've reached a cheery voice on the phone, the voice of a woman who had no idea she was going to ever come home to see what she was seeing.

I've reached the voicemail of a woman whose last name was somewhat familiar. An unusual last name. Who did I know with that name? I disconnect before the tone can sound. The dispatch center is buzzing quite a bit with words like "Did you page so and so?" and "What if Channel 5 calls again?" It was a terrible and unusual call, I figure, but newsworthy?

Someone behind me asks, "Were you talking to the mom on that suicidal?"

It is a street supervisor.

"I didn't have it very long," I say. "Are they transporting?" (That is my way of asking if she might still make it.)

"That's Roy Treech's daughter," he says. One of our street medics.

The medic whose name sounded so familiar was on duty and in another rig in the same county when he heard his ex-wife's address dispatched on the radio. That's how he found out. On a beautiful, sunny summer day in Minnesota. One of the first really good ones that year. That is how he found out that his daughter had shot herself.

For the last half of my last twelve-hour shift, my last shift ever as a 911 dispatcher, I mourn a sixteen-year-old girl along with my colleagues.

There is no celebration and there are no funny memories anyone can think of, and everyone but me forgets it is my last day.

As I wrap the cord neatly around my headset for the last time, I know that I will never bond like this, never suffer like this, never feel as glued-together by another group of coworkers, ever. I will never need to cling to another group of otherwise strangers as though we have all been in the same plane crash together. I will never feel so connected in such an unusual and oddly familiar way. I will probably never feel as high as I can feel in this job, or as low.

On my way out the door, I hug everyone who will let me. I linger until I feel awkward. I leave my security badge with Luke and send a group good-bye e-mail.

~

I now work in an office as a technical writer. My head is generally on my pillow no later than 10:00 P.M., and I'm up by 5:30 A.M., just like a regular Joe. My first few weeks on the job, I fought the urge to ask permission before almost every trip I made to the restroom.

I write about machines. Big machines that make boxes, fill boxes, and then seal those boxes. It is, on some days, darned interesting. It is, on some days, boring as shit. Nothing I do has any kind of life-or-death consequence. Nobody ever says, "You're a technical writer? *I bet you've got some good stories.*"

Every once in a while, I catch a news story about a dispatcher who made a difference. Every once in a while, I catch a news story about a dispatcher who fucked up, and is catching hell.

I am sad that I'm no longer making a difference, but I wonder how long it would have taken for me to really catch hell.

I am grateful to have made a difference.

I am grateful to never have known.

Acknowledgments

I played a lot of softball as a kid, and my dad volunteered as third base coach for most games. Dad was a third base optimist. If I or any of my teammates made it to second base, you could almost guarantee he was going to wave you through. "Atta way!" he'd yell, gesturing wildly with his whole body. "Come on, come on, here you go, that's it!"

You made it this far, kid. Keep going. You've got this.

I learned the truth about that later, when Dad confessed, "I knew if they [the other team] tried to make the play, nine times out of ten, they couldn't make that throw. It's just too far to third base. Nine times outta ten!" Okay, so it was less about his belief in us, and more about his lack of faith in the other team's abilities.

No matter.

I am forever grateful to my parents, Richard and Audrey, who have been my lifelong third base coaches, wildly waving me through to the next thing with constant love and support, whether they understand it or not, whether they love it or not. I love you both so very much.

I am grateful to the soft-spoken and eternally lovely Ann Regan, editor in chief at MNHS Press, and The One Who Discovered Me. If diplomatic editing and tasteful suggesting were award categories recognized by the Academy, Ann would have a cabinet full of little gold statues.

I am grateful to MNHS Press. To be offered a book contract with a good, sturdy, reputable publishing house was more than I'd ever really dared to hope for in one lifetime. Two books? Craziness.

To Shannon Pennefeather of MNHS Press, for her thoughtful edits and ideas. Also, thank you in advance for letting me steal your awesome last name for my next novel.

To my daughter Mariah, and to my dear friends Chrissy, Chad, and Jill, who should each receive a special royalty for every time they had to endure me whining that I really should be writing right now.

To Tama and Jen, for contributing their memories and being adorable.

To Aimee and Barth, for their help with that one chapter that about killed me.

Finally, I send my love and gratitude to all of the dispatchers who worked with me, trained me, fed me, carried me, and made me part of the 911 family over the years. You provide a service that we can't live without. You are not forgotten.

You've made it this far. Keep going. You've got this.

Printed in the USA
CPSIA information can be obtained
at www.ICGtesting.com
JSHW082206140824
68134JS00014B/463